Pastoral
Care
of
the
Handicapped

Pastoral Care of the Handicapped

Roy E. Hartbauer, Editor

 Andrews University Press, Berrien Springs, Michigan

Dedication

This book is dedicated to my wife, Joyce, and her parents, Dr. and Mrs. Vernon E. Hendershot, who by precept and example demonstrate compassion as the manifestation of God's love.

—R. E. Hartbauer

Copyright © 1983 by
Andrews University Press

Published February 1983 by
Andrews University Press
Berrien Springs, MI 49104

ISBN 0-943872-87-1
Library of Congress Catalog Card Number: 82-74357

iv

Contents

CONTENTS

Contributing Authors

Darold F. Bigger, Ph.D., is pastor of the Walla Walla College Church in College Place, Washington. He holds degrees in theology from Walla Walla College and the Seventh-day Adventist Theological Seminary at Andrews University, and in theology and personality with emphasis on counseling from the School of Theology at Claremont, California. He was director of the Christian Counseling Center in Riverside, California. He is a Fellow of the American Association of Pastoral Counselors, Clinical Member of the American Association for Marriage and Family Therapy, and is licensed by the State of California as a marriage, family, and child counselor.

Roger H. Ferris, M.A., is pastor and marriage counselor of the Volunteer Park Seventh-day Adventist Church in Seattle, Washington. He has academic degrees from Atlantic Union College, South Lancaster, Massachusetts; in applied theology from the Seventh-day Adventist Theological Seminary at Andrews University; and is presently a candidate for the Ed.D. in religious education and family from the Department of Education at Andrews University. His other publications include *The Couple Workbook: Communication Skills in Marriage* and *Christian Family Literature in the '70s*.

Lorraine Guild-Smith, Ph.D., is coordinator for and in charge of development of aging education courses and curricula for Lake Michigan College's Human Services Program. She has academic degrees in reading from Andrews University and in adult education, reading, and gerontology from the University of Michigan. She is co-leader for the Region IV White House Conference on Aging, 1981 delegate to the State White House Conference on Aging, a member of the Education

Task Force for Widowed Persons Service, and a task force member of the Berrien County Hospice Program.

Roy E. Hartbauer, Ph.D., is professor and chairman of the Department of Communicative Disorders, director of the Speech and Hearing Clinic, and coordinator of the learning disabilities program at Andrews University. He holds academic degrees in theology from Walla Walla College, College Place, Washington; in speech from the University of Southern California, Los Angeles, California; and in audiology and speech science from Michigan State University, East Lansing, Michigan. Additional studies have been in vocational rehabilitation and counseling. He is a member of the American Speech, Language, and Hearing Association, from which he has certificates of clinical competence in both speech-language pathology and audiology, and is also a member of the American Auditory Society, the Society of Medical Audiology, and the Michigan Speech, Language, and Hearing Association. His publications include *Aural Habilitation: A Total Approach* and *Counseling in Communicative Disorders.*

Thomsen U. Kay, M.A., is coordinator of services for the deaf at the Christian Record Braille Foundation, Lincoln, Nebraska. He has academic degrees in religion and education from Oakwood College, Huntsville, Alabama, and Ohio State University. He belongs to the National Association for the Deaf, Lincoln Register of Interpreters, Professional Alliance of Businessmen, and National Register of Interpreters for the Deaf.

Donald A. Riesen, B.A., has been for the past eight years the director of pastoral care at the Florida Hospital in Orlando, Florida. His interest in hospital chaplaincy resulted from his assignment as pastor of the Sanitarium Church on the grounds of the Florida Hospital the previous four years. His thirty years of pastoral ministry include pastorates in Philadelphia, Toledo, Minneapolis, and Chicago. He has a Bachelor of Arts degree from Columbia Union College. Graduate studies have taken him to Andrews University, Berrien Springs, Michigan; Loma Linda University Medical Center, Loma Linda, California; and Harding Hospital, Worthington, Ohio.

John Treolo, B.S., is assistant director of public relations for the Christian Record Braille Foundation, Lincoln, Nebraska. He has academic degrees in public relations from Pacific Union College, Angwin, California, and Canada College in Redwood City, California. He is a member of the Public Relations Society of America.

John K. Umeda, D.Min., is a chaplain at the Veterans Administration's Brentwood Medical Center, Los Angeles, California. He has academic degrees in applied theology from the Seventh-day Adventist Theological Seminary at Andrews University; in counseling from California State University, Hayward, California; and in ministry from the School of Theology at Claremont, California. He is a licensed marriage, family, and child counselor in the State of California.

Preface

During the initial stages of the development of this book the writer contacted a chaplain of a hospital in a large city in the western United States. The chaplain was invited to participate in the writing of this book. The reply was, "Oh, I wrote a pamphlet some years ago on helping the handicapped, and there really is no need for anything more. It isn't that important." The follow-up conversation revealed that he apparently did not have a concept of working with the over 50 million handicapped in America. He apparently was not interested in finding out more about working with them.

In contrast to this, almost all other clergymen contacted were eager to learn more about the handicapped and how to work with them. They mentioned that they probably had preconceptions that were not right, that they had prejudices, fears, apprehensions, and that they were ignorant of the problems and lives of this significant minority. One pastor said, "I am frightened when I come in contact with a handicapped person because I am afraid I will do something wrong." Other ministers have said they feel the same way. Still another minister confessed, "I am anxious to find out what I have been missing. I guess I've been too busy 'being a preacher'."

With this introduction let us take a look at what is involved in pastoral counseling of the handicapped. We will see that it is both a separate ministry and a ministry that is part of a larger whole. It is a ministry that is not for every pastor just as surely as public evangelism or youth work or large (or small) city ministry is not for everyone. Hopefully, you will learn more about yourself.

While working with the handicapped the pastor deals with many things. There is the unknown. To begin with, there will be many things unknown to the pastor about each of the handicaps, its causes, symptoms, and effects. Many things are unknown to the patient and to those close to him. There are unknowns in the health care field, as evidenced by the tremendous amount of relevant research. There are unknowns about how a specific individual or his body will react to rehabilitative procedures. And the greatest unknown is how God will choose to intervene. You, as a pastor, will be called upon to try to explain the working of God in the realm of the unknown. You will be expected to explain the how and why of the handicap in the light of special relationships you, as a minister, have with God. These are mysteries of God and godliness that we will never know.

Because of the nature of sin and the need of man to admit his guilt in order to accept the saving life of Christ, there are many facets of guilt for the pastor-counselor to understand. Throughout this book there is much discussion about separating out guilt associated with sin, *per se*, guilt connected with the real cause of a handicap, the guilt we borrow needlessly, and the guilt other people impose upon us. The pastor will find that this is one of the major problems with which he must deal.

Another concern is that of interference, primarily from third parties. Nearly every experienced clergyman has wished that interference in his plans and planning would disappear. With the handicapped, interference comes from parents (sometimes only the father or the mother), other relatives (including either know-it-all or uninformed sons or daughters), other health field personnel, pastors who have a different faith or orientation than yours, red tape, and, on occasion, from the patient himself. It would be impossible to mention all the sources of possible interference. Suffice it to say that once they are identified, they are easier to handle and resolve.

Next we turn to a problem that can complicate and/or even underlie all others. It is what is commonly called "breakdown in communication." The purists in the field of communication maintain that it is impossible to "not communicate." They believe that we are carrying on some communication or communicating something at all times. Let us therefore refer to the breakdown of intended or desired communication. Your knowledge of the pastor's role in care of the handicapped and your growth in that role prevents much of that breakdown. Be it connotative or denotative, verbal or non-verbal, encoding or decoding, intellectual or emotional, there can be satisfactory communication. It is one of the pastor's tasks to help keep the channels open. He is an interpreter, buffer, transliterator, translator, and friend. He is trusted and distrusted. He is believed to be anything from someone knowledgeable to even someone "way out in left field." He is the one who asks some people to cease talking while urging others to talk more. The pastor is the one to whom it is said, "O.K., preacher man, you know all the answers; you have a direct line to God." He may be called upon early or late—hopefully the former. He is called upon by some who feel that his word is "the word of the Lord."

As we look in a different direction we can ask, "What is human nature?" Furthermore, we can ask, "What is abnormal human nature?" "Can these be separated from human behavior?" "How far do we let behavior deviate from 'normal' before we consider it a disorder or a contributor to a disorder?" It is possibly best for this discussion to define human nature as the way the person reacts intellectually and emotionally in both routine and emergency (stress) situations. It is his thoughts and feelings and how they are translated into action or words. Our human natures are as individual and distinct as fingerprints. The presence of a handicap makes that individuality even more unique. The pastoral role is to help the person establish or reestablish a functional human nature and/or form a human nature with which he is comfortable. We must always be aware that we are not dealing with inanimate objects, non-feeling, non-thinking animals, nor super creatures. We are dealing with human beings.

Added to all those things discussed above, the pastor-counselor deals with the entire constellation of the handicapped. Spouses, children, parents, associates in social, occupational, and recreational pursuits, and other persons influencing the handicapped are all part of their constellation. Each additional person in the constellation adds more than one more dimension. It is not a simple addition of one. Each person must interact with each other person and those interactions are altered by each additional member. Identifying each interaction and attempting to understand it could consume all of the pastor's time and prevent his dealing with weightier matters. Strangely, some members of the constellation can create interactions strictly for the pastor to see. They are mere smoke screens with no other purpose than to avoid unpleasant or unwanted factors and facets. Ideally, the pastor-counselor will spot these diversions and quickly label them as such.

Next, the pastor is on the horns of a dilemma in that he must ask himself if he should deliberately influence the client's values; and if so, which values and in what way? Does the client want his values changed? Has the handicap forced him into looking at his own sets of values—religious, health, social, professional? Have his strayings from his values learned, or at least taught, during his childhood contributed to the handicap? At times of trauma the individual is receptive to having his values changed. As observed by a study of the Guyana tragedy, people proved to have great gullibility in times of distress and lost their lives as a result.

Should the pastor see wisdom in attempting to change a handicapped person's values, he must honor the right of the counselee to accept or reject the pastor's proposals. The handicapped person has the right to develop his own code of ethics and philosophy of life, and to live with the consequences.

Lastly, we are to remind ourselves that pastors counseling the handicapped deal with all kinds of attitudes toward religion. Concepts of a Supreme Being are numberless and coexist with the concept that there is no Supreme Being. Dealing with this is the pastor's greatest challenge. Ultimately we need to acknowledge that the pastor is involved because it is his vocation and personal and professional commitment to merge himself into the spiritual foundation of each life.

TYPES OF HANDICAPS

Handicaps can be broadly divided into three groups: (a) skeleto-muscular anomalies, (b) sensory deprivation, and (c) mental-emotional problems.

The skeleto-muscular group can be further subdivided into: (1) abnormal structure, (2) abnormal functioning and paralysis, and (3) lack or loss of body part due to congenital factors, accident, or surgical intervention.

Sensory deprivations that are customarily considered as handicaps are loss of sight and loss of hearing. The loss of the senses of taste, smell, and feeling is most frequently handled as an inconvenience. Perhaps this is true because these senses are not temporal or spatial as are seeing and hearing; neither are they so critical for communication or cognitive learning.

The mental and emotional group can be subdivided into: 1) disorientation in time, space, and reality, and 2) non-coping with life on a daily basis or in emergencies even though the general orientation is within normal limits. It is this last group that can be a handicap by itself or be a companion to any other. Gradually, theological seminaries are including training in this area. This is one of the purposes of this book.

THE PASTOR'S NEEDS IN COUNSELING THE HANDICAPPED

There are "tools" the pastor-counselor needs that come basically from without himself. They include: information regarding handicaps, formal training, literature for himself and client, and referral sources. These can be acquired. Hopefully this book provides them.

Within himself the pastor needs to find open-mindedness, receptiveness, flexibility, emotional and psychological stability, and compassion. We, as writers, cannot give these to you. We offer only lighted mirrors for self-exploration and self-discovery and lighted pathways for exploration of the experiences of others. The working of God the Father, God the Son, and God the Holy Spirit is within the knowledge and expertise of the pastor himself.

Note must be made that all the contributors to this book realize that both male and female pastors are involved in counseling the handicapped. Rather than using a cumbersome "he/she", the generic "he" is used with absolutely no intent of discrimination for either counselor or counselee.

Roy E. Hartbauer

1

Understanding the Pastor's Role in Ministering to the Handicapped

The pastor is frequently called upon at a time of urgency, such as trauma, or may be called upon during the period following trauma. The trauma of which we are speaking is the onset or discovery of a handicap. At that moment the person and/or his constellation around him are confused, fearful of both the known and the unknown, depressed with many feelings of hopelessness, bewildered with wondering "why" and with the shattering of their dreams. Their lives take on different characteristics and meanings and must be viewed with changed perspectives. The aims, goals, objectives, and purpose of life must be reevaluated. Priorities must be reappointed. The pastor is called upon as a support person because he supposedly has insight, has probably helped others through similar sloughs of despair, and because, in the eyes of some people, he has "an inside track to heaven." It must be our prayer that our lives and commitments to God in reality are so close and so strong that we are worthy of this belief so that God can use us.

The pastor is to help the patient and his family (constellation) from two viewpoints: first, the effects of the handicap on the patient,

1

and second, the social, economic, emotional, occupational effects and interpersonal relationships within the family. Underlying all other concerns are the questions the pastor must help answer: "Why did this happen to us/me? Where did it come from? Is there a God, and if so, why did He let this happen?" They call upon you because they feel *you* have all the answers, *you* can explain God and His ways, *you* can "call on God" because *you* are considered a representative of God.

They will also call upon you because they can use you in several ways. They may use you as a true source of strength, as someone who can answer sincere questions, someone upon whom they can lean, or someone who they know will listen and accept them as they are without praise or condemnation. Or, they may use you as someone whom they can attack, someone they may try to blame.

All of these factors force the pastor into asking some questions of himself: Who am I? What am I to do? and How do I do it?

First, what are the qualifications I must have to actually be a counselor of the handicapped?

Some of the criteria are identical at first glance to those that must be yours as a pastor. Yet, they take on different perspectives when you counsel concerning handicaps. The perspective changes because you are adding another dimension to the questions you face in day-by-day parish visitation. All the common concerns are still there but they have a different urgency; various things must be looked at here and now. There is a greater depth of conviction that the person's relationship to God and his concepts of temporal and eternal life be considered without delay.

The pastor must realize that both intellectual and emotional factors must be pursued in their changed conditions as reapportioned by a handicap. The calling you have had to the ministry and your criteria have not changed, but your qualifications, from both training and experience, are viewed through a different prism in the presence of a handicap.

Now for some specifics. Before counseling the patient, you, as a pastor, must evaluate yourself. First, know the depth of your own religious faith and conviction. This depth determines the extent of your service. A superficial faith becomes more shallow when counseling the handicapped. Do not be deceived into thinking that a shallow faith is not observable. Know, first, the Lord Jesus Christ. Know whether in your own heart and mind you truly believe the things you say. Know if you fully comprehend the scriptural references you use. Are they merely texts which you can use as escape routes? Are the texts a gimmick that says, "That's what the Bible says, so don't ask any more questions"? Search deeply for the full import of the inspired writings. Study the contexts, contents, and intents. Evaluate the value and the fulfillment you have had both directly and vicariously by applying them to unique situations. Become aware of the specific applications of passages rather than using all texts in a shotgun manner.

Before counseling the handicapped, ask yourself if you really believe the promises and prophecies. Have you felt a change in your life that shows God the Father, God the Son is real? The continuous living experience of a deep faith is the first prerequisite of a pastoral counselor of the handicapped.

Next, have no selfish strings attached while counseling the handicapped. Perhaps the perceptive reader has known a pastor who continued in his position without a total commitment to that specific type of Christian ministry. Some pastors can fall into the trap of feeling the pastoral role is easy, or prestigious, or is a protection against numerous forces that they feel they would have to confront without the shield of being called a pastor.

Do not allow your pastoral counseling to be a tool that could ultimately lead to untenable situations. Likewise, do not let your ministerial office be a device for attempting counseling for which you have no qualifications. Avoid the feeling of superiority because you are the pastor and other persons are not. You are called to this place for such a time as this, just as are all the others involved in the patient's care.

The sole motive of pastoring to the handicapped must be to promote the physical, mental, emotional, and spiritual welfare of the patient. There is no place in the scheme for the pastor to feel selfish motives, other than the fulfillment of a special ministry commitment. You counsel for the benefit of the patient. We all recognize that there are tremendous rewards that come to the pastor, but these are not the reason for his ministry. Among the rewards are seeing the development of the patient's belief in God, beholding the outpouring of the blessings of Christ, the Master Healer, and seeing positive changes in the patient and in one's self.

Now let us consider the qualification of recognizing your limitations with a determination to strengthen yourself. For example, the writer feels he is a bigger man for admitting that other speech/language pathologists and audiologists are more successful than he is with preschool children, while feeling a strength with other types of clients. No one can be all things to all people. The pastor should not try to be.

As a professional person identifies and accepts his limitations, it frees him to search for answers to questions that may arise when his pastoral services are requested regarding new/different handicaps that he has not faced previously. Most beginning pastors, and uncounted experienced pastors, have not been confronted by situations any more trying than have their parishioners. However, preparation for the possibility of these experiences is wise. It is well to have a library with specific information about specific handicaps. At times the element of immediacy may militate against referring to those sources, but usually there is at least enough time to have a brief review of the problem, its causes, and possible directions to go.

Along with these qualifications, know yourself. Perhaps this is markedly difficult because it is so broad. Let us break it down by asking ourselves certain questions. How do I react toward someone with a visible deformity? Am I typical in that I react only mildly toward someone with affliction of the lower extremities and body and more markedly to someone with an affliction involving the face and head? Can I objectively discuss the handicap with the patient, his health care team, and his constellation of family and associations? Do I have any feelings of repulsion from the handicapped? Do I know the ways and means by which I would face the problem if it were mine? And, can I work with this patient as a whole person?

Hopefully, we are beyond selective, negative reactions to different types of handicaps and do not categorize some handicaps as more repulsive than others. We must be able to objectively discuss the loss of a limb, loss of functioning, loss of sense modality, or disfigurement with the health care professional in terms that are within each discipline. A knowledge of technical terminology will help us understand the case from a broader perspective. We must be equally able to discuss these things with the family and, most importantly, with the patient, in lay terms.

We should know what intellectual and emotional reserves are available within ourselves. Said another way, we must have an idea of our inner strengths and psychological stability. We must have an integration of mental, spiritual, and physical resources and control of them in emergency and traumatic situations.

Along with these qualifications must be the ability to extend acceptance to the handicapped. Accept the person as he/she is. That is the starting point. We are destroying him if we continue to think of him and react to him as he was before the onset of his handicap. And, it is impossible to accept him as he will be. Today, at this moment, this person is exactly as he is. Accept him, even to perhaps having to help him accept himself. Of course, a knowledge of the "here and now" facilitates acceptance. Even without full knowledge, however, accept that which is available.

Part of accepting is letting the person express his feelings of doubt, fear, anger, hostility, disbelief, confusion, shattered hopes and plans, anxieties, and basic reactions. We are not to condemn people for telling the truth. We must let people express their thoughts and feelings of the moment. We must not shut down a person's innermost integrity in the hour of crisis. We are only kidding ourselves if we say to him, "Now, now, you don't really feel that way." It is likely that the person has either momentary or long-standing doubts about the attributes of God. Let him express them and explain them; then handle them at the correct time. Pastors hear language in the hours of trouble which is not the customary language of the speaker. Accept it as his use of tools of expression while under intense stress.

We will hear confessions and rehearsals of things the person has done that are not in accordance with God's law. It may be that this is the moment when he finally feels he can discuss them and feel a purging from the experience. The individual is not trying to shock you. He is not giving you an opportunity to vicariously relive his sins. He is asking for and needing acceptance, not condemnation nor commendation. He is asking for and expecting acceptance rather than judgment.

A turning point came in the writer's life when he realized that God does not want us to come to His throne in sorrow when we sing the song, "Just As I Am". It is a song of joy and excitement that you have found out about the acceptance that is yours through Christ. It is to be sung with tears of rejoicing, not with tears of self-flagellation. Extend this type of acceptance to those who need it. The more you have discovered the acceptance of God in your own life, the more you can give it to others.

Following the acceptance comes the time to start to redirect the person's life. Acceptance is the starting place. As a teenager once told me, "You can't tell someone how to get to San Francisco unless you know where he is starting." So it is with your counselee. As you are familiar with his feelings, thoughts, and physical being you can start to give him guidance for self-direction.

Accept the person who has recently acquired his handicap and the stage of grief, as Elisabeth Kübler-Ross calls it, or the "stage of self preservation," as this writer calls it, that the person is in. Accept the reality that everything *is not* all right. Accept the person with his long-standing handicap and the technique, procedures, and devices that he has been using in maintaining who and what he is.

All through the handicapped person's life there is a tension be-tween acceptance and resistance. This tension is an ongoing affective state. The person accepts the handicap while resisting it with various degrees of resolve to fight it.

The pastor's role is largely one of listening. He is to encourage the handicapped to speak openly and freely about everything that is bur-densome as well as speak the joys and victories the person has ex-perienced. We listen to find out how he/she is coping. And, we listen to find out how much the handicapped have in common with the unafflicted.

Pastoral listening involves the complicated process of noting, at-tending to, and perceiving someone else's verbal and nonverbal com-munication. Through listening we create perceptual sets and attributes that influence both the amount and kind of material we receive from the handicapped and our responses to that material. We can feel one way one minute and another way the next minute during the listening process.

The pastor-counselor role is to listen first, understand, and then formulate and test hypotheses. As Christians we believe that God listens when we preach, sing, and pray. We believe that He hears our songs and our prayers and that He understands us. It is impossible as humans, however, to completely forget self and listen completely to someone else as does God.

This goes along with formulating and testing hypotheses. As we listen we are constantly to put into our own words what the handi-capped person is saying, putting one point of discussion against another. The listener must note similarities shared by humans in their experiences and in their emotions. Some writers refer to the experiences of the emotions—love, happiness, hurt, pleasure, loneliness, ac-complishments, and so on.

Hypotheses are tentative beliefs or approaches that you feel the af-flicted can try. Later they are to be accepted or rejected. Either way they are building blocks.

CAPITALIZING ON THE POWER OF THE WILL

Along with listening, the pastor's role is one of reinforcing the will to live. This may be an exhaustive search for possibilities for survival, encouraging participation in a legitimate medical experiment, or psychological, mental, emotional, and spiritual counseling to lessen a feeling of helplessness and hopelessness.

Experienced pastors who have worked in rehabilitation settings know the challenge of keeping up the morale of the seriously impaired. If you have not had such exposure, you are urged to visit a rehabilitation center for a period of time to observe the activities of the members of the rehabilitation team. You will see how dependent the staff is upon the patient's own will to live and how critical is the patient's responsiveness to the encouragement given by each professional. The more responsive the patient, the more successful the rehabilitation. Handicapped people with a strong will to live are more cooperative with the people who are helping them. Note that this is, in itself, a great reward to the helpers.

It is worth attention that psychologists have found that the afflicted who have a firm, active religious faith as a reservoir are more hopeful than persons who do not. Numerous doctors have observed the importance of a vital belief in a Supreme Being.

The pastor-counselor may be less involved in direct modification of behavior, yet as a member of the team he can do much to reward desired behavior and eliminate or reduce the opportunities for the undesirable. From Transactional Analysis we can borrow the concept of giving "strokes" to persons who are participating in the appropriate way. These "strokes" are words of encouragement, expressions of understanding what the counselee is communicating, and a reassuring touch.

As Americans, we seem too averse to touching. This is a tragedy in our society at large but an even greater tragedy while dealing with the handicapped. The writer has seen numerous incidents of fear of touching the disfigured, the mentally impaired, and the physically handicapped. People seem to fear that any abnormality may be contagious, and an uninformed, unsure, insecure pastor is no exception. People will recoil from the hug of a handicapped child—just the thing a child badly needs. The writer has seen people brush themselves off after physical contact with the "abnormal" person. A genuine holding of hands, pat on the shoulder, hug, or appropriate kiss is very often the communication that is needed. We cannot justifiably continue to ridicule or laugh at the caste system in India with its untouchables when we have within us a tinge of the same thing. We are being hypocritical when we approve of a back rub but will not give the same touch of love to another part of the person, such as the arm, leg, face, or hand.

The legitimate question arises, "Isn't there a chance that I will physically hurt the patient-counselee?" If you have sufficient commitment to your pastoral care you will learn *how* to touch and such a fear will cease. A tragedy is that some pastors do not even know how to shake hands. There is no personal touch to their handshake. Some, after the church service, give a handshake that pulls the people past them. Some squeeze too hard and hurt the hands of the feeble and arthritic, and some have the "dead fish" handshake. The handicapped have felt all these before and read them better than the rest of us.

Let us not overlook the "religious strokes." Do not get the idea that this is used in a derogatory way. Neither are we at this time referring to systematic, in-depth, and wise religious instruction and guidance. Religious strokes can be superficial. Recently the writer heard of a hospital chaplain who prided himself in seeing every patient in a good-sized hospital every day. He stated that with this routine he had no time for any other pastoral counseling. His routine was to walk up to each patient, read a scripture, pray for the patient, and leave. His "strokes" were superficial and resented by numerous patients.

Let's now look at his procedure. First, he never got to know each patient nor the reason for the hospitalization and could not recognize him/her on sight anywhere else. Next, he never let the patients get acquainted with him enough to see inside his heart and mind. Third, he projected the image of a man more interested in form and formality than in truly caring for the patients. Next, he gave good grounds for people to question the Christian commitment of the hospital and even to laugh at him behind his back. Lastly, he deprived himself of the reward that longer, less frequent visits can give.

Another type of "stroke" that is not desirable is the use of flip expressions, such as: "Everything will be all right;" "It is God's will;" and "Let us pray about it." These are frequently used when the pastor has nothing more appropriate. Do not think that any of these expressions is not to be used. Rather, we are noting that they can be used inappropriately.

At this time we might be wise to question what types of prayers are to be given when the handicapped person is on the gurney and is being wheeled to surgery. If he is there because of an accident that will result in a handicap, he is in deep trauma and a lengthy prayer is out of place. If he has been sedated for surgery being done as a rehabilitative procedure, he is unable to comprehend an involved prayer. The same is true while he is returning from the operating room. If you must pray at these times, keep your supplications brief and simple. The patient will be able to comprehend that you are there and that God's care is being requested.

ENCOURAGING SEXUAL NORMALITY

Next we are going to discuss a frequently avoided topic: the sexual wholeness of the handicapped. Fortunately it is not so avoided as it was in the past. Charles Wittschiebe set the tone for the thinking of one denomination by the title of his book: *God Created Sex*. His design was to discuss sex in accordance with biblical teachings as a beautiful, normal, and rewarding facet of God's creation. There are some minor parts of his discussion with which the reader may disagree, but there can be agreement that sex is part of God's plan of human communication between husband and wife.

In their counseling, pastors should ask, "Does God deprive the handicapped of this part of life?" "Should the handicapped feel guilty for desiring sexual compatibility and activity?" God does not deprive a person of a sex drive just because there is some other structural or physiological problem. Society has been inclined to assign a "no sex" placement to the handicapped in the strata of the culture and when something involving sex and the handicapped is known, the response is either to feel that it is terrible, negative, and degenerate, or to laugh. It is true that laughing serves as a discharge of feelings in a way that society will accept. We laugh (if that is what you call it) at what we don't understand.

The handicapped are not incorporated into sex education classes in some settings. Or, they are assumed to be getting some of their sex education off the street like the non-handicapped do, yet they do not. Less than five years ago a young adult told the writer that she (a nineteen-year-old at the time) was ridiculed and scorned for asking some basic questions. She was deaf and had not received either formal, guided sex education or the "street" training. Readers are directed to the paperback, *In This Sign*. The book is set in the depression days but the deaf of today verify that much of what happened in this story based on a true experience is going on *now*.

What does this have to do with the pastor? If the handicapped get involved in a sex-related problem and the pastor has not helped them view sex in a wholesome perspective, he is a major contributor to the problem. If the handicapped participate in normal, moral sex lives and feel guilty and we have not told them it is all right, then the guilt is actually ours.

The amputee, the partially paralyzed, the person with a communicative disorder, or the sensory deprived—deaf or blind—is entitled to a healthy sexual self-concept. Eliminate unfounded guilt. Give them normal, God-sent, whole, sexually-satisfied self images. Few pastors are equipped to give sex education and possibly they should not be, but they can complement such instruction by being competent, stable, and well-adjusted persons. Urge the handicapped and give guidance toward expecting a wholesome sex life which God has put within.

THE "PASTOR" ROLE IN PASTORAL CARE
OF THE HANDICAPPED

You have been trained in theology; you have been trained in exegesis, homiletics, hermeneutics, biblical criticism, expository preaching, church management, financing the church, fund raising, home visitation, and filling out your monthly report. You may have even had some clinical pastoral education training, but no formal training in working with the handicapped. For point of inquiry you question, "Is there a real difference when it comes to the handicapped?" There definitely is, because of the added ingredient— the handicap. For the sake of a starting point, let's notice the similarities between those who are handicapped and those who are not.

The handicapped can be: (a) active, devout church members, (b) passive church members, (c) devout searching persons, (d) rebellious church members, (e) atheists.

What has been the handicapped person's attitude toward God in light of the handicap? Has it been a sincere question or a hostile challenge when he asked, "Why has this happened to me, God?" Has he shown a faith in divine guidance or has he been bitter when he said, "God has a reason"? Has it been a firm conviction or a resolution to accept God's vengeance when he states, "It is all part of God's plan"? The parents of handicapped children, too, are challenged by these feelings and attitudes. A compassionate pastor is compelled to let the person say what he feels toward God at that moment, or as he relives the moments from the past. We are compelled to *accept* him and his feelings. And it is ultimately critical that *at this time we do not judge.* To do so is to turn him off, to bring guilt (or in some cases inappropriate self-righteous feelings) and to place in his mind the idea that we desire the "right" attitudes and feelings more than the true. After we start judging we may get a distorted picture, because the person may start to paint what he thinks we want to see. Do not be misled. There is a proper time to deal with "right" and "wrong", but it is *not* while the person is first trying to sort things out. Well-meaning clergy and friends say such things as, "You don't really mean that!" or "You're just under strain and you don't honestly feel like that, now do you?" The fact is the person *does* mean what is said and *does* feel that way. It is normal to have feelings and thoughts. And it is normal to resent being told that you don't feel and think as you have stated. The "pastor" role expects you to be understanding of a person's feelings toward God in times of trauma.

Pastor-counselors daily find parishioners who rationalize, excuse themselves and their actions, or employ numerous devices as "cop-outs." As you work with handicapped they may "use" either their handicap or their religion as a rationalization or "cop-out" for the other. Of course, there are many times that there is a legitimate connection between the handicap and a change in religious behavior. For example, there may be a real hearing loss that makes attending church services a tribulation. Do not confuse this with a loss of interest in a worship experience. Think of the preacher who says, "I have my way of speaking and I don't have any plans to change just because there is someone who is deaf in my congregation." Contrast that with the minister who says, "Thanks for telling me. I'll be more careful to stand so he can see me and read my lips, and I'll be sure there is nothing in front of my mouth." No one can blame the parishioner in the first illustration for staying away from church because of the hearing impairment and the preacher's attitude.

On the other hand, there are people who say in a pseudo-martyr way, "This is my terrible burden that God has given me to bear. Oh, it is so heavy, but I must struggle on." They use their handicaps to obtain pity. They use them to say that "God has given me this and He will lead me by Himself." They close their ears to religious counseling. The pastor may have the task of telling these people that they have incorrect beliefs in God and His mysterious ways. It is no easy process to tell someone his belief in God is not right, yet to have him keep his faith in God. The pastor has to have within himself a clear vision of God's workings.

Our next topic of discussion on the role of pastors centers on the individual and/or family who have been long-standing members of the pastor's own church affiliation. Perhaps they have just recently faced the reality of a new handicap. Or, perhaps there has been a long-standing handicap but now the family members bring, or let, the pastor into the circle.

Regardless of whether the handicapped persons were reared in the church or evangelized into the church in later years, the rapport of common beliefs is a springboard for pastoral counseling. The common beliefs eliminate much of the "feeling each other out" process, but do not eliminate it entirely. The pastor needs to determine what is known and what is believed. Find out why they believe, but more importantly, find out the experiences behind their lack of belief. Understanding the events associated with the unbelief gives directions to follow in leading into belief. Frequently guilt is a companion to the nonbelief. There is guilt connected to the onset of the handicap, guilt that the events have been a stumbling block to belief, and guilt for not believing. We cannot overemphasize the need to eliminate guilt, either by encouraging confession to God and acceptance of His forgiveness or by showing the irrelevancy of the guilt.

Different problems confront the pastor-counselor when the handicapped is a member of another denomination and is searching for a more complete Christian life. Where does a pastor begin? Begin where you would with a nonhandicapped person. Recently the writer was counseling with a 28-year-old woman who was partially disoriented. She had a medical diagnosis of some brain damage due to use of street drugs. During the third session she expressed a desire to pray but said it had been so long that she had forgotten how, and she was not even sure which saint she should employ. She had been reared as a Roman Catholic. The writer, as a Protestant, believes that prayers should be spoken directly to God rather than through saints, the Virgin Mother, or other mediators. What should be done? Was this a golden opportunity to teach the difference? Was this the moment for a Bible study? In no way. The woman was guided to pray a simple, earnest prayer that was comfortable for her. The prayer she gave brought tears to everyone in the room, and we felt she had taken us all closer to God. The prayer was, "My Jesus-God, I am sick and I hurt. I need to talk to You more. I know You can make me better. Please. Amen." There could have been no better prayer. She began where she was. She renewed her identification of and with God. There can be no greater common ground than your agreement with every word of her supplication. Many follow-ups can be built upon that.

Find the common beliefs in an omnipotent, omniscient, and omnipresent God, in reconciliation through the blood of Christ, and in our salvation through the life of Christ (Romans 5:10), and relate them to the handicapped. Find the common belief in the Holy Spirit, the Ten Commandment law of God, and justification by faith. Start with the existing compatibility. Christ perceived where his listeners were and used their belief in the promised Redeemer as the foundation upon which he built. Pastors have the same responsibility and opportunity. Christ did more miracles for the handicapped than for anyone else. Twenty-five of His thirty-five miracles dealt with those persons who would today be called handicapped.

THE "UN-ROLE" OF THE PASTOR

In November 1978 a tragedy took place that shook the world. Nearly a thousand people participated in a mass suicide in Guyana on the word of their religious leader. Prior to that event he had completely imprisoned their minds and their wills. He had directed their devotion to himself and his teachings rather than to the God whom he professed to represent. He did not want them to live without him nor did he want to live without them. The latter, strange as it sounds, would have been the easier of the two. Parenthetically, we note that this attitude on the part of the leader is one of the characteristics of a cult which differentiates it from a fundamental religion based on worship of a Supreme Being.

This attitude is also a characteristic of the minister—the missionary in particular—who must build his program around himself. He builds programs that are designed to collapse if he should leave. This collapse would demonstrate just how irreplaceable the leader is. This attitude is not limited to religious leaders. A careful reading of a best seller of a decade ago, *The Ugly American*, will reveal that diplomats and ambassadors do the same thing.

The process begins with the adulation and praise that is given to every leader. It becomes food for an ego that cannot be satisfied with anything less than total exaltation. We must admit that there is a need for praise in each of us, but it must be monitored. It is an absolute must that we have an ego that finds greater fulfillment in having our counselees becoming self-sufficient and self-directed *without* us. Of course, this requires a life centered upon God. The emotionally, psychologically, spiritually healthy person is the one whom we have helped live *without* us. We are destroying the individual whom we train to depend upon us for all decisions and directions. We are not speaking of the intermediate goal of getting someone to lean on us while he is learning to exist alone; rather, we are discussing the moving beyond the temporary phase. Do not let the temporary become permanent.

Some writers refer to the client's *self-actualization*. The counseling pastor is part of a team with this goal. *Self-actualization* is both an intermediate and an ultimate goal. It goes beyond living with a handicap, disorder, dysfunction, illness, or whatever you wish to call it. Self-actualization has to do with achieving a whole life, including spiritual life, without you, the pastor.

Self-actualization is not static, but dynamic. It is a basic human motive. Maslow did a study that brought out fourteen characteristics of the self-actualized person:

1.   Efficient perception of reality and comfortable relation to it.
2.   Acceptance of self, others, and nature
3.   Spontaneity
4.   Problem-centering (focus on problems outside the self
5.   The quality of detachment; the need for privacy
6.   Autonomy; independence of culture and environment
7.   Continued freshness of appreciation
8.   Experience of ecstacy, awe, and wonder
9.   Deep feelings of empathy, sympathy, or compassion
10.   Deep interpersonal relationships with others
11.   Democratic character structure.
12.   Ability to distinguish means from ends
13.   Philosophical, unhostile sense of humor
14.   Creativeness

The discussion of self-actualization is part of the discussion of goals. The handicapped *do* want to achieve educational levels for full utilization of their own potential. They *do* want to obtain employment. They *do* want to have a marital status which is right for them (including saving or terminating a marriage). They want to overcome obstacles to their personal growth, achieve optimum development of personal resources, attain a clear sense of personal identity, accept limitations, achieve interpersonal relationships, and control their own personal environment. The handicapped want to do all this ultimately *without* your help. When this is accomplished, you are to happily step back and let them be on their own. No greater honor can be bestowed upon you than that your counselee can finally live without you. You have worked with him until he no longer needs or wants your help. Be big enough to rejoice with that moment.

Finally, we come to the role of congregational liaison for the handicapped. The pastor's role is expanded to counseling every member of the congregation in how to relate to the afflicted. In fact, it also may involve other ministers. Pastors aren't the only people who don't know how to associate with the handicapped. The narthex of your church may witness a silence falling upon people when a handicapped person enters. It has seen people indicate that the handicapped are to be allowed to sit only in selected areas of the sanctuary.

During conversation, members of your churches may make cutting remarks to and about the handicapped. Examples are: "You are in this condition because of your sins." "I would talk with you more but I have some important people I am trying to impress." "Wouldn't it be better if this person were institutionalized and away from people?"

Two years ago the writer's daughter was waiting for her sister in a large airport. A group of about a dozen very alive deaf teenagers were carrying on an animated and vocal discussion with much laughter. They were using sign language as part of their communication. A very sanctimonious late-middle-aged woman arrived with her entourage and upon noticing the group stuck up her nose and said, "That sort of person should not be allowed to be seen in public places," and, literally tightening her coat around her, walked several paces away. The writer's daughter went over to the woman and told her that she needed pity for her ignorance and cloak of self-righteousness. The brief discussion that ensued at best helped the woman to realize that thinking people have a more wholesome attitude toward vibrant youth who have something different about them. Such remarks as the woman's are made in many churches, too.

What is the pastor to do? Here are seven suggestions for helping the handicapped:

1. Identify what the church must do for the physical well-being of the handicapped. Arrange comfortable and convenient seating. Be sure that barriers are removed. Be sure that restroom facilities are accessible.

2. Arrange transportation to services.

3. Appoint responsible church members as companions, guides, interpreters during services.

4. Introduce the handicapped to each other.

5. Give a sermon, or a series of sermons, emphasizing the points in this book. Most of these points can be as effectively used by the non-pastor as by the pastor.

6. Present the handicapped to the congregation

as whole people in the love and in the eyes of
God.

7.   Remind the congregation that the handicapped
are alive seven days a week and welcome,
deserve, and need Christian fellowship for more
than the 11:00 to 12:00 hour once a week.

Before you there lies a way. This discussion portrays the pastor in
many roles; fill each role. Then when God asks, "Where are *all* the
beautiful sheep?" you can say of the handicapped, "Here they are, Lord."

BIBLIOGRAPHY

Argle, M. "The Syntaxes of Bodily Communication." In *The Body as a Medium
of Expression*. Edited by J. Benthall and T. Plhemus. New York: E. P. Dutton, 1975.

Ban, Thomas A., and Lehmann, Henry E. *Experimental Approaches to
Psychiatric Diagnosis*. Springfield, Ill.: Charles C. Thomas, 1971.

Barsch, R. *Counseling with Parents of Emotionally Disturbed Children*. Springfield, Ill.: Charles C. Thomas, 1970.

Benjamin, A. *The Helping Interview*. Boston: Houghton-Mifflin, 1974.

Berne, Eric. *Games People Play*. New York: Grove Press, 1964.

Bird, Brian. *Talking with Patients*. Philadelphia: Lippincott Co., 1973.

Cobb, A. Beatrix. *Special Problems in Rehabilitation*. Springfield, Ill.: Charles
C. Thomas, 1974.

Cox, Richard H. *Religious Systems and Psychotherapy*. Springfield, Ill.:
Charles C. Thomas, 1973.

Cull, John G., and Hardy, Richard. *Counseling Strategies with Special Populations*. Springfield, Ill.: Charles C. Thomas, 1975.

Dawidoff, Donald J. *The Malpractice of Psychiatrists*. Springfield, Ill.: Charles
C. Thomas, 1973.

Delapp, Mary. "An Experiential Worship Encounter." *Pastoral Psychology* 22
(March 1971):212.

Feifel, Herman, ed. *New Meanings of Death*. New York: McGraw-Hill Book
Co., 1977.

Hiltner, Seward. *Preface to Pastoral Theology*. New York: Abingdon Press,
1958.

Kahn, R., and Caunell, C. *The Dynamics of Interviewing*. New York: John
Wiley and Sons, Inc., 1959.

Leslie, Robert C. *Sharing Groups in the Church*. Nashville: Abingdon, 1970.

Mikesell, William H. *Counseling for Ministers*. North Quincy, Ill.: Christopher
Books, 1961.

Mooney, Thomas O.; Cole, Theodore M.; and Chilgran, Richard. *Sexual Options
for Paraplegics and Quadriplegics*. Boston: Little, Brown, and Co., 1975.

Murphy, A. "Parent Counseling and Exceptionality: From Creative Insecurity to Increased Humanness." In *Professional Approaches with Parents of Handicapped Children*. Edited by E. Webster. Springfield, Ill.: Charles C. Thomas, 1976.

Nouwen, Henri J. F. *Creative Ministry*. New York: Doubleday & Co., 1971.

O'Brien, Michael J. *An Introduction to Pastoral Counseling*. Staten Island, N.Y.: Alba House, 1968.

Oden, Thomas C., et al. *After Therapy What?* Springfield, Ill.: Charles C. Thomas, 1974.

Pond, Desmond. *Counseling in Religion and Psychiatry*. London: Oxford University Press, 1973.

Satir, Virginia. *Peoplemaking*. Palo Alto, Calif.: Science and Behavior Books, Inc., 1972.

Schaller, Lyle E. *The Pastor and the People*. Nashville: Abingdon Press, 1973.

Slovenko, Ralph. *Psychotherapy, Confidentiality and Privileged Communication*. Springfield, Ill.: Charles C. Thomas, 1966.

Vanderpool, James A. *Person to Person: A Handbook for Pastoral Counseling*. New York: Doubleday & Co., 1977.

Wise, Carroll A. *The Meaning of Pastoral Care*. New York: Harper & Row Publishers, 1968.

Roy E. Hartbauer

2
The Counselee

The writers would be remiss if we did not give a discussion of the counselee in the process of counseling the handicapped. When psychotherapy or counseling is being done, the client's voluntary participation in the sessions is a basic requisite. He must believe that there will be a change in him. In the counseling of the handicapped the same would be ideal. However, this belief is not always present when the pastor enters the picture. Counselees can be anything from highly motivated with great expectations to improperly motivated with no desire to change. The latter individual may be receiving some unique nurture from the sympathy, pity, and attention received and may not want to forfeit it.

The handicapped counselee must be ready and willing to use time, money, and intellectual and emotional strengths. Realistically, we note that some of this readiness may be slow in coming, particularly when the counselee does not know for sure what is going on, is unsure of the pastor, or has had a disappointing or bitter previous experience. Too many people have had unpleasant contacts and confrontations with clergymen.

Some handicapped need to have their belief in a pastor cultivated from a small seed. They need to believe in a counselor-pastor to whom they can express all their feelings and attitudes and to whom they can confide their intimate and personal experiences. They need to let the pastor "inside." The pastor cannot get in without the individual opening up his feelings and emotions.

The client must have faith in the pastor and absolute faith that what is said will be kept confidential. The handicapped may have been through it all before and may be more perceptive of the many factors of a counselor-counselee interrelationship than are many others.

If he has a pastor in whom he has ultimate faith, the handicapped person is willing and able to involve himself in self-disclosure, or as some call it, self-exposure. He will and must make himself vulnerable. He does this by self-exploration with an observer (the pastor) present. He brings to the front all the negative aspects of his problems, inadequacies, failures, and undesired feelings. Because of what the pastor has lived and "died" with, he may have heard all these negatives before. Now he must have them presented from within the handicapped. Beginning pastors are concerned over how much they should attend to this self-abnegation. There is a critical difference between encouraging or even rewarding the counselee for his introspective excoriation and listening with acceptance to the person who speaks of depression, discouragement, unworthiness, and, on occasions, thoughts of suicide. The individual needs to know that he is not weird, sinful, or to be exiled for having such thoughts and feelings. We listen to help him see the normal aspects of life and to pass from the negative to the positive reserves he has within himself. He needs to have it pointed out that the "wrong" of a negative self-concept comes from dwelling upon it. Self exploration assists in finding what needs to be changed. The client cannot change something until he knows what it is.

The following story should illustrate the point. A traveler phoned an information center and asked for directions to a certain place. The person asked him, "Where are you now?" The traveler responded with a question, "That doesn't make any difference, does it?" We laugh at this because it is so ludicrous, yet we do not realize that people do the same thing regarding requests for self-help. We must help them find out where they are and then we can help them make the desired progress.

While some have no difficulty with rapid self-exploration, others must go more slowly. Most counselors prefer to explore in depth one area at a time, while doing shallow work in others. It is not necessary to exhaust one area before moving on.

During the client's self-exploration, the pastor is to determine if there are any discrepancies between the client's "self" as viewed by others and his own image of "self", between what the person says about himself and his behavior, and between what the person says about himself and what you, the pastor, observe. If there are discrepancies, we must ask why. They can either be diversionary movements or motivated by many reasons.

In time, the counselee should come to accept himself. He should emerge with a positive self-concept. Every handicapped person should seek to claim this as his possession. He is to learn that there is a more competent, positive, adventurous, and capable self under the cover he has removed. He has to say, "I am all right. I'm worth putting some effort into. I deserve the positive things I am getting." Now before someone says that we are not to love ourselves, let us look at Christ's words when he said, "Love thy neighbor as thyself." We cannot love others until we love ourselves *in Christ*. This points out that we are to feel good about ourselves, that we are to enjoy our lives, that we are to identify and use the good points about ourselves. We are to care for ourselves as God's children and consider ourselves to be worthwhile, just as Christ considers each of us worth enough to die and to live for us. We are discussing *self-worthiness*, not *selfishness*. As Christians we are compelled to recognize and encourage the self-worth of the handicapped.

Counseling changes the client into a free person. He is free *to be himself*, free to explore his potential, free of hatred, anger, frustration, hostility, fear, unwarranted limitations; and with pastoral counseling he is free from guilt. He is released from playing roles, previous conditioning, and unnecessary inhibitions. He is no longer the same person. An ancient philosopher once said, "You can't step into the same river twice." Neither can a man be unchanged by interpersonal relations with a pastor-counselor-friend.

SELF-PRESERVATION

One of the sermons the writer gives begins with asking everyone in the congregation who is a sinner to raise his hand. Usually a large percentage of the hands are raised. The next statements are, "I'm so sorry. I really don't believe that you are sinners." The sermon then develops the concept that when we accept Christ as our Savior we are no longer sinners; rather, we are "sinners saved by grace." Notice the difference that Christ makes. We are new persons in Jesus Christ. We are free from guilt for all our sins of the past. We are to free the handicapped from the past, as well.

Guilt is a terrible load; yet both ministers as individuals and denominations as corporate bodies have "used" guilt to control their people. People have been conditioned to feel guilt and get crushed by guilt. The handicapped are no exception.

The handicapped go through the guilt phase in a process similar to mourning. Kübler-Ross has developed the "mourning theory" that people go through at the death of a loved one. The writer has developed what he calls "phases in self-preservation." The first phase is *truth rejection*. Kübler-Ross calls her first step *denial*. In truth rejection the individual, upon hearing bad news, says, "No, it can't be true;" "You're kidding;" or "You're making that up." It is news that he does not want to accept and believe. He starts to put together all the evidence that the statement cannot possibly be true. The person who acquires a handicap goes through this phase initially in spite of the hard, cold facts. For example, let us use the case of a person whose hearing has deteriorated to a handicapping level. Audiologists see people who (1) declare, "My hearing is all right; other people just don't talk as plainly as they used to;" (2) monopolize a conversation so they do not have to listen; (3) establish a repartée that sustains them; (4) become recluses to eliminate the need to listen; or (5) even outright lie about what they think they can or cannot hear. The amputee, the paralyzed, or the disfigured has no comparable "out."

If the handicap has been present from childhood there is little reason to believe that the truth rejection phase was significant. On the other hand, some handicapped people go through this phase in learning that some new medication, appliance, or procedure cannot do what was hoped. They want to say, "But it *will* work." Parenthetically, this same human trait of truth rejection coupled with eternal hope is worked on by the purveyor of "sure cures," "miracle drugs," "new inventions," and other "medicine man" products.

Truth rejection is an instinct in the parent who learns that he/she has a handicapped child. It is repeated when the parent finds that nothing miraculous can be done about it. Parents respond with, "It couldn't happen to me," or, "Oh, no, not *my* child." It is not uncommon that parents, and more often fathers, reject the child along with rejecting the diagnosis. Fathers will reject sons if the infants do not fit into a preconceived idea of what "my son" is going to be like, especially if the father has an image of an athlete or a so-called "real he-man." It appears that the father instinct is not as strong as the mother instinct when it has to do with accepting and rearing handicapped children.

In another form of rejection, one parent who accepts the child and the responsibility will hear from the spouse, "Either me or the kid, but not both. Either you ship that kid off and give your ministration to me or get out." Here we have a major ego problem in the one making the ultimatum. Doubtlessly, that person would be nothing but an additional handicap to the child and a barrier to its development.

Grandparents can reject both truth and the child. The grand-parents' rejection filters down in a manner established long before the birth of the child. The birth of a handicapped child does not alter family attitudes and approaches to life, but it does magnify them or bring them to the surface.

From the *truth rejection* phase, mourners—that is, people in cataclysmic experiences—go into the *responsibility acceptance* phase. Kübler-Ross states that the second step is *guilt*. The writer feels that *responsibility acceptance* is a more inclusive and dynamic way of viewing this part of the process. At the moment of tragedy, after truth can no longer be rejected, the person turns inward. Before he even asks, "Is it my fault?" or, "Could I have done more?" he puts his thoughts and feelings as statements. He "knows" that the fault is his, that he could have done more to prevent the handicap. He judges himself guilty by both commission and omission. He tears himself open and sees the wrong in his life. He starts to reason that all this would not have happened if he had not lived an "immoral" life, had not lived with abandon, or had been more faithful in doing such and such. People go searching for additional things to feel guilty about. They borrow trouble. They incorporate irrelevancies.

The perceptual eyes are not seeing clearly at this time and it is difficult to sort out the legitimate causes of the problem for which people feel responsible. As vision clears they finally sort it all out. The pastor-counselor must also know the causes of the handicaps to be able to guide the person in sorting out what is and is not causally related. Especially, the person who acquired his handicap after childhood has to do this sorting out. He has to understand that some handicaps afflict people when there is no possible way that they could have prevented it. He has to have acceptance of *no* responsibility. To illustrate this concept we have the case of a pressman who had the lower part of an arm severed in a cutter due to no fault of his own. He had done everything according to safety guidelines. It was after the disaster that it was discovered that another workman had bypassed a safety device. The handicapped printer had to accept his innocence.

The introspection of parents with a handicapped child is extremely harsh. They feel an even greater measure of guilt-responsibility because of what is happening to their child. Nearly every parent has said, "If this could have only happened to me instead of to my child." The handicapped person must relate to the parents' feelings, too.

The parent *should* accept the responsibility only if he: (1) has been responsible for an accident; (2) has not followed instructions, procedures or protocol in administering medicines; (3) has been criminally negligent or violent; (4) has contracted by immoral action a disease that afflicts the child; or (5) has prevented others from caring for the child.

What does the handicapped person need from the pastor during the responsibility-accepting stage? He wants the pastor to guide him in segregating out the real from the imagined or borrowed. He wants the pastor to help him ask for forgiveness. All sins can be forgiven by God and the pastor must help the guilty person believe in God's forgiveness. The pastor is to point out that it shows distrust in God when we ask repeatedly for forgiveness for the same sin. The word of God says, "If we confess . . . He will forgive." Ask once, believe, and move on. Do not give credence to any idea of atonement by the individual or of doing penance. Christ atones for us. Offer to the handicapped the responsibility of accepting God's gift of love. This is needed by the afflicted.

The third phase in self-preservation is *suicide potential*. The counselee who has had good experiences through the first two phases slips through the third without difficulty. Others turn their anger inward and feel "all is lost." They rationalize that there is no more effective method of eliminating pain, guilt, ridicule, rejection, or being burdens to others than self-destruction. They have self-pity and self-abnegation. They feel a crushed omnipotence, yet reason that they would regain that omnipotency by having absolute control over their own deaths. When they have lived with a problem as long as they feel they can bear, they seek the escape route of suicide.

The handicapped person needs alternatives. He needs to see that there are other ways out. Do not say, "It is not as bad as you think." That statement only shows that you are unaware of the counselee's perspective at the moment. To him, at that instant, it *is* bad. He needs to know there are ways of resolving or getting rid of the bad. He needs a different perspective. Find out what his ego strengths are. Give him criteria for evaluating. When his mind is focused on these things the self-torture, depression, and death wish will disappear.

An alternative to self-destruction is to attempt to destroy someone else. That brings us to phase four—*aggression*. Pastors should not take the aggression directed against them as personal. The counselee is striking out in self-defense and uses anyone available. He may attack you and want you to "solve this mess." If you try to solve it and fail, then he can logically say you are no good. If you do solve it, he can say that you are no good because you did not let him solve it himself.

Look at the case of a child with a hereditary handicap, particularly one that skips generations. One parent can blame the spouse and "your family's genes" for the disorder, whether it is true or not. Placing the blame on the other spouse is a form of aggression. While there is nothing wrong with identifying facts, it leads to no good when it is regarded as "blame." The "blame" can be placed on the other person for real or imagined mistreatment of the child, disagreement over management, or marital infidelity. There are fewer cases of unhealthy and unfounded aggression by the handicapped themselves than by the nonhandicapped.

Lastly we come to phase five—*habilitative participation*. When all other phases are behind, the handicapped and/or all others involved in the process will find this to be the best and most exciting phase. The counselee is ready to do what he must. He has a positive self-image. He relates to both his strengths and his limitations. He sees progress that he has not seen before. Hopefully there will be growth and positive, dynamic change for the rest of his life. The pastor's role shifts and reshapes. He grows with the handicapped whom he now cares for with Christian love.

BIBLIOGRAPHY

Ban, Thomas A., and Lehmann, Henry E. *Experimental Approaches to Psychiatric Diagnosis.* Springfield, Ill.: Charles C. Thomas, 1971.

Benjamin, A. *The Helping Interview.* Boston: Houghton-Mifflin, 1974.

Berne, Eric. *Games People Play.* New York: Grove Press, 1964.

Bingham, Walter, and Moore, B. *How to Interview.* New York: Harper and Brothers, 1959.

Bird, Brian. *Talking with Patients.* Philadelphia: Lippincott Co., 1973.

Cobb, A. Beatrix. *Special Problems in Rehabilitation.* Springfield, Ill.: Charles C. Thomas, 1974.

Cox, Richard H. *Religious Systems and Psychotherapy.* Springfield, Ill.: Charles C. Thomas, 1973.

Cull, John G., and Hardy, Richard. *Counseling Strategies with Special Populations.* Springfield, Ill.: Charles C. Thomas, 1975.

Feifel, Herman (ed.). *New Meanings of Death.* New York: McGraw-Hill Book Co., 1977.

Hartbauer, R. E. *Counseling in Communicative Disorders.* Springfield, Ill.: Charles C. Thomas, 1978.

Iwin, R. B. *A Speech Pathologist Talks to Parents and Teachers.* Pittsburgh: Stanwix House, 1962.

Kahn, R., and Caunell, C. *The Dynamics of Interviewing.* New York: John Wiley and Sons, Inc., 1959.

King, Rella R., and Berger, Kenneth W. *Diagnostic Assessment and Counseling Techniques for Speech Pathologists and Audiologists.* Pittsburgh: Stanwix House, 1971.

Mash, E.; Handy, L.; and Hammerlynck, L. *Behavior Modification Approaches to Parenting.* New York: Brunner/Mazel, 1976.

McDonald, E. *Understand Those Feelings.* Pittsburgh: Stanwix House, 1962.

Messer, Alfred A. *The Individual in His Family: An Adaptational Study.* Springfield, Ill.: Charles C. Thomas, 1970.

Mooney, Thomas O.; Cole, Theodore M.; and Chilgran, Richard. *Sexual Options for Paraplegics and Quadriplegics.* Boston: Little, Brown, and Co., 1975.

Oden, Thomas C., et al. *After Therapy What?* Springfield, Ill: Charles C. Thomas, 1974.

Slovenko, Ralph. *Psychotherapy, Confidentiality and Privileged Communication.* Springfield, Ill.: Charles C. Thomas, 1966.

Wilson, D.; Genott, H.; and Gerges, S. "Group Interview: Initial Parent Contact." *Journal of Speech and Hearing Disorders* 24 (1959).

John K. Umeda

3

When There Has Been a Stroke

A stroke leaves the patient with disabilities so devastating physically, mentally, and psychologically that the emotional reactions to the experience are intense. Further, his impairment has a far-reaching psycho-social impact on the family of which he is a member. No wonder a stroke is aptly called "the illness of the family." The stroke not only disables the patient, but also in a sense paralyzes the whole family system, leaving it in a disturbed and disrupted state.

When the stroke victim is the breadwinner, his/her dysfunction threatens the livelihood of the family. To enable the family to survive this adverse situation, the partner assumes the responsibility of supporting the family in addition to carrying on housekeeping tasks. Often the burden and responsibility of caring for the victim after his/her return from the hospital makes role adjustment or reversal of the partner difficult, if not impossible.

Stroke patients and their families in such crisis need all the professional help available to accomplish recovery and rehabilitation. Because of his symbolic role as a representative of a church and as a "confessor" or father figure, a pastor can be of invaluable help to the stroke patient. In cooperation with other professional team members he can provide the patient the necessary support through counseling, which will enable him to cope with the illness more positively and constructively.

In view of the complexity and nature of the illness, the pastoral counseling of stroke patients requires more than mere expertise in the art of counseling. For a pastor to be successful in counseling the stroke patient, he must have an adequate grasp of the psychological effects of brain damage due to stroke so he will understand the patient's behaviors in their proper context. This background knowledge will also enable the pastor to be in touch with the "here-and-now" of the stroke patient by understanding his emotions, which result from his reactions to his disabilities.

POSSIBLE ETIOLOGIES

The term "stroke" (cerebrovascular accident, CVA) describes the results of any cause which prevents an adequate amount of blood from reaching a section of the brain, causing the death of brain cells. Fifteen to twenty percent of strokes are caused by cerebral embolism. This is a condition in which a small clot of blood circulating in the bloodstream lodges in one of the tiny blood vessels in the brain, and the stoppage of blood flow to the nerve cells in this area of the brain causes these cells to die. The number of cells which die depends on the size of the plugged vessel.

A more common cause of stroke is a cerebral thrombosis, which accounts for seventy to seventy-five percent of all strokes. This condition is caused by coagulation of the blood in some part of the circulatory system, forming a clot which stops circulation in that part. The result is the same as in the case of cerebral embolism.

Approximately five to fifteen percent of strokes are caused by brain hemorrhage from a broken blood vessel. This condition results in the loss of oxygen supply to the cells beyond the break, and causes the build-up of pressure on cells in the area surrounding the break. When blood escapes from the broken vessel, it quickly closes the break by forming a clot and thus stops the hemorrhage. Later the clot is absorbed, and the pressure is relieved. Then some of the cells temporarily deprived of oxygen may be able to function again.

DESCRIPTION AND DETAIL OF HANDICAP[1]

Though it varies with individuals, almost all spontaneous recovery takes place within the first three to six months. Spontaneous recovery is

---

[1]The author is indebted to Roy S. Fowler, Jr., Ph.D., and W. E. Fordyce, Ph.D., for their booklet entitled *Stroke: Why Do They Behave That Way?* in writing this section.

that which comes about by the body caring for itself as opposed to the recovery that results from rehabilitative procedures. It occurs when the swelling (edema) around the damaged area which interferes with brain function clears up or the bleeding is absorbed. The recovery is partial because the larger affected area of the brain recovers but there is a smaller dead part that will be replaced by scars.

Most improvement of intellectual or functional deficits is demonstrated during the first three to six months. After this healing period is past, the problems will remain relatively unchanged, and as the time increases from the onset of the stroke, the percentage of return of these functions diminishes.

The effects of the stroke on the person depend on the number, kind, and location of brain cells that are damaged by the temporary lack of blood supply. A stroke patient with damage to the left hemisphere of the brain is likely to have paralysis of the right side of the body and an accompanying condition called aphasia. This is a speech and language problem with a total or partial loss of power to use or understand language. Speech and comprehension are not necessarily both impaired, however. An aphasic stroke patient who cannot express himself appropriately is not necessarily unable to comprehend the speech of others. This is evidenced by the fact that many aphasic patients quickly develop effective communication skills without the use of speech by resorting to gestures and unusual sounds.

Therefore, by quickly assuming that the patient does not understand speech and treating him accordingly, we can hurt, harm, and do disservice to him. Daylong (p. 128) makes a very important observation in this respect. He points out the tendency of persons around the patient to speak to one another about him, as if he were not present. This is annoying to the patient and convinces him that there is no one who will listen to him, causing him a great feeling of isolation from the social environment of which he is a part. Daylong further states that such treatment deprives the patient of the social stimulus necessary to increase his verbal abilities.

There is another characteristic of the right hemiplegic which needs to be understood. There is a tendency to be anxious, cautious, slow, and disorganized when learning new self-help activities such as dressing or transferring from the bed to the wheelchair. This hesitant behavior may come as a surprise to those who knew the patient previously. Those who attend to him should exercise patience and understanding, and adapt the instructions to his condition so that he will not be made to feel insulted or humiliated.

Left hemisphere brain damage may also cause regression and sudden personality changes in the stroke patient. He becomes childish in behavior and emotionally unstable, cries easily and frequently, and demands immediate attention.

On the other hand, a stroke patient with damage to the right hemisphere of the brain is likely to have a paralysis on the left side of the body (left hemiplegia). Characteristic of the left hemiplegic is difficulty with spatial perceptual tasks, namely, the ability to judge size, position, distance, rate of movement, form, and the relation of parts to the whole. These spatial-perceptual problems pertain to simple self-care activities, such as bringing food to the mouth or reading the newspaper without losing the lines. The patient feels frustrated over his problems, but he may appear as uncooperative, unmotivated, overly dependent, or confused to those who do not understand him.

The left hemiplegic is also characterized by his tendency to be impulsive and hasty, and frequently may try to do things which are beyond his abilities or unsafe. For example, he may try to walk across the room without putting on his braces.

A problem which occurs in both right and left hemiplegics, but seems to be more prevalent among left hemiplegics, is the difficulty of seeing objects to the left of the center of the visual field. Most stroke patients learn to compensate for this visual field cut by turning their heads to see if they have missed something, but there are some who do not seem to make this adjustment. This one-sided visual field cut, in addition to the numbness of the impaired side of the body, affects the way the stroke patient perceives things and causes varied problems of neglect. This is often manifest in the way the patient grooms himself and fastens his clothing.

These are some problems associated with paralysis on one side of the body or the other. Some patients will give no evidence of paralysis, and yet will give signs of the disabilities mentioned so far. Others will show paralysis but little or no evidence of these other problems.

A stroke patient, in general, has problems in quality control, which refers to the ability to correctly interpret the environment and respond to it in the most appropriate manner. Such quality control or social judgment enables a person to regulate his behavior so he may conduct himself properly. Therefore, a patient with this problem may become sloppy and seem to be careless about his appearance. He may say the wrong thing at the wrong time.

Memory problems are quite common among the brain-damaged, such as the stroke patient. The right hemiplegic tends to have more memory difficulties in dealing with language, and the left hemiplegic, in relation to spatial-perceptual tasks. It is also possible to have neither language nor spatial-perceptual problems and still have significant memory disabilities.

Memory has many components. An important component is retention span. A stroke patient often has a short retention span; therefore, the number of pieces of information in any given message he can retain and use or act upon is limited. This is the reason why instructions given to the stroke patient needs to be in short, simple sentences.

Memory also involves old or new learning. Old learning refers to information acquired prior to the stroke, and new learning to information acquired since the stroke. Because of this factor in memory, a stroke patient may have difficulty remembering instructions or appointments but may be able to describe in detail events which occurred many years in the past.

A stroke patient with memory problems also has difficulty in generalization—that is, carrying over learning from one setting to another. Therefore, a change in environment which requires adjustment or adaptation is frightening to the patient with this disability. He may become irritable and confused in reaction to these changes. Consequently, a deterioration in ability should be expected when there is a change in environment.

One of the most striking features of the personality changes observed in stroke patients is loss of control over the emotions, commonly called emotional lability. The patient suffering from such lability may weep, laugh, or appear angry without intending to do so. Or, with the slightest provocation, such as being greeted by the physician, nurses, or friends, the patient may cry for no reason. He may stop crying just as suddenly as he began.

These sudden outbursts of emotions are baffling to the patient as well as to those around him. This behavior can have a very shocking and frightening effect on those who witness it without understanding its cause. Thus there is a tendency for the family, the friends, and the pastor to avoid the patient for fear of another occurrence. The result is further isolation of the patient from the social contacts he needs more than ever before. A stroke patient is already suffering from sensory deprivation, a condition in which stimulation from the outside world has decreased significantly. Patients in this condition are lonely, and become restless, confused, and irritable.

COMPREHENSIVE REHABILITATION PROGRAM

The following section describes a comprehensive rehabilitation program for stroke patients. It is intended to give the pastor an overview of the program so he will know how to judge when and where, in the process of the patient's recovery, his pastoral counseling can be of greatest value.

Stroke rehabilitation may be defined as the process of helping the patient recover from the psychological effects and neurological dysfunction resulting from the stroke. Though the outcome of rehabilitation for each individual is unpredictable, 99.9 percent of stroke patients will not recover completely, but will probably have some degree of residual physical and mental deficits to live with for the rest of their lives. Therefore, the goal of rehabilitation is to help the stroke patient make the transition from sudden illness to independent community living by offering long-term suport so he can accept his disabilities and develop a new way of life.

Each stroke patient has the potential to optimally recover from or cope with the mental and physical effects of stroke. The full realization of this potential requires the services which the interdiciplinary team provides. In a hospital setting this professional team consists of a physician (either a specialist in physical medicine, a neurologist, or a general practitioner experienced in the treatment of stroke patients), a nursing team, a physical therapist, an occupational therapist, a social worker, a psychologist, a public health nurse, a speech pathologist, and a chaplain. Other special therapists may be involved as indicated; for example, in art, music, dance, and re-socialization.

The diagnostic evaluation is the vital first step in the treatment of the stroke patient. Its purpose is to determine the presence of: (1) any condition other than stroke which is causing the neurologic symptoms; (2) treatable conditions specifically causing stroke; and (3) conditions which aggravate or increase the risk of stroke, such as hypertension and diabetes mellitus (Jones, p. 178). This initial diagnostic evaluation helps the staff to determine an appropriate treatment and establish realistic rehabilitation goals as early as possible.

Sahs and his colleagues list the following objectives of stroke rehabilitation (see chapter bibliography):

> (1) To prevent or minimize secondary complications such as contractures, infections, . . . or effects of disuse which may interfere with natural recovery of function; . . .

(2) To compensate for sensory loss which can result in a variety of secondary deficits such as inability to walk effectively or to judge whether the body is upright;

(3) To encourage social participation and to provide the environmental stimulation needed for recovery;

(4) To enable the patient to achieve maximal psychological integration and stability;

(5) To produce the high degree of motivation necessary for successful cooperation in a rehabilitation program;

(6) To substitute for a function impaired or lost, once the level of recovery has been estimated or anticipated;

(7) To enable independent home living, or, if this is impossible, to attain improvement in the patient's condition sufficient to permit his future care with the least possible amount of assistance and supervision;

(8) To achieve, in some cases, sufficient vocational rehabilitation to enable placement of the patient in competitive employment or in a sheltered workshop;

(9) To provide a level of communicative skills adequate for establishing and maintaining interpersonal relationships.

It can be seen that pastoral counseling will be most effective in helping the stroke patient meet the third, fourth, and fifth objectives of the rehabilitation program.

PASTORAL APPROACHES

One of the most difficult counseling situations a pastor will ever run across is the counseling of stroke patients. This is due to the brain damage which causes physical and mental or psychological disabilities with profound and far-reaching emotional and social effects in their influences on the patient's mental outlook and life style. For example, a pastor will be at a loss to respond appropriately to an aphasic patient who cannot express himself understandably or to one who has sudden emotional outbursts due to emotional lability. Under such circumstances counseling a stroke patient may turn into a frustrating and embarrassing experience unless the pastor understands the organic origin of these difficulties and develops an effective approach.

The best approach to counseling a stroke patient lies not so much in what a pastor may say or do as in the quality and the kind of relationship he brings to the counseling process. The implications and meanings of this therapeutic relationship for counseling the stroke patient are also vitally important.

As in any counseling situation, pastoral counseling must have a starting point. The pastor initiates this relationship with the stroke patient when he introduces himself as a pastor. However, the introduction is unnecessary if the patient is one of his parishioners.

The early establishment of such a pastor-patient relationship is crucial for pastoral counseling because it determines the nature and quality of the continuing therapeutic relationship which the pastor and patient have with each other. However, it is the pastor who gives significance to this relationship by his symbolic role. He represents to the patient the church and all spiritual and religious values. He projects a loving and protective father image, which ultimately points to the loving Heavenly Father. In this symbolic role the pastor is a very significant person to the stroke patient. Thus, the counseling relationship will help the stroke patient in his crisis to maintain a supportive relationship with a "significant other," and, in turn, will help strengthen his relationship with God.

Another element the pastor brings to the counseling relationship is empathetic understanding of the stroke patient. This empathetic understanding must be born of an intellectual grasp of the physical and mental disabilities associated with cerebral damage due to a stroke and their effects on the patient's mental outlook, emotions, social and family relationships, and life style.

In order to relate appropriately to each patient, the pastor needs to familiarize himself with the present condition of the patient and the stage of recovery he is in. The pastor must free himself of preconceived ideas and be able to enter into the counseling process with all the awareness and sensitivity he possesses so the patient may sense that the pastor understands him and is with him.

The counseling relationship also requires, on the part of the counselor, "a genuine interest in and concern for the client (patient), a strong desire to help him, to influence or change him" (Patterson). Whatever the goals of pastoral counseling for the stroke patient might be, the effectiveness of counseling depends on the ability of the pastor to zero into and touch the heart of the patient. Therefore, the pastor brings his whole being to bear upon the counseling relationship; he gives to the patient his whole, undivided attention, the best gift he can bestow on him. The implication of this is that the patient is important and deserves the pastor's complete attention.

The pastor becomes an incarnate love of God by the way he relates to the patient. He accepts the patient just as he is regardless of his problems and difficulties or his disagreeable characteristics, without being judgmental. In addition to unconditional acceptance and non-judgmental attitude, the two important ingredients in pastoral counseling, the pastor expresses another dimension of God's love by his *commitment* to the patient. Beginning with the initial interview and in the following sessions the pastor conveys his commitment to provide a sustaining support to the patient.

The outcome of all these expressions of love is the establishment of a trusting and loving relationship. In this kind of relationship the patient will see the pastor as someone he can confide in; consequently the sharing of his disturbing thoughts and feelings becomes natural. Moreover, the pastor will be successful in motivating the patient to give his full cooperation to the rehabilitation program.

EDUCATING PATIENTS AND FAMILIES

The importance of the pastor's having an adequate background knowledge of stroke for counseling cannot be overemphasized. The stroke patients and their families need to have just as much knowledge so they can understand what is going on and be able to cooperate with the rehabilitation program.

So often patients and families have a poor understanding about the extent of the patient's disabilities. The revelation of the extent of disabilities is traumatic and the patients and families have difficulty accepting this. The hope of being able to do things independently is the most important motivating factor for stroke patients, and nobody wants to shatter it. However, this hope must be realistic in view of the fact that some dysfunctions are permanent and normal functions are unrestorable. Functions which will compensate for these disabilities need training in order for stroke victims to achieve some degree of independence. On the other hand, some patients can wait for temporary dysfunctions to clear up spontaneously to some extent, depending on the nature and extent of the brain damage, so that they can cooperate with a subsequent training program to obtain optimum recovery for independent living. At any rate, they need someone who can explain to them in layman's terms the facts about stroke and reinforce the information given by other team members.

The pastor is an ideal member of the team to fulfill this function, in cooperation and consultation with the physician and other team members. The pastor should ascertain how much the patient and his family understand of what is going on by asking questions. This will help the pastor to know what knowledge to impart. In the supportive relationship of the counseling sessions the pastor can gradually impart and reinforce relevant information to the patients and their families.

PATIENT'S EMOTIONAL AND INTELLECTUAL REACTIONS

The most basic emotional reaction to the physical and mental deficits that result from a stroke is fear. Charatan and Fisk enumerate four causes of fear on the part of the stroke patient (p. 1403):

"Fear of being left permanently crippled and handicapped." The stroke patient looks into the future with fear because permanent disability means losing control of his situation and remaining helpless the rest of his life. Such fear is not imaginary but real to one who is presently experiencing physical and mental deficits and may not be improving after the spontaneous recovery period of three months is past.

"Fear of another stroke." The patient who has had a stroke can never rid himself of the fear in the back of his mind that he may have another one which can inflict more damage or may mean his death.

"Fear of impoverishment." A stroke reduces an independent, often gainfully employed person to one totally dependent on others, and possibly financially depleted if he has been hospitalized with a subsequent lengthy period of convalescence.

"Fear of loss of love." The stroke patient has a sneaking suspicion that his loved ones will not love him the way he is now. The stroke patient feels he is a burden to his family and also feels unsightly because of facial paralysis, excessive drooling, or muscle contractures.

Such fear is very real and seems too much for any person to tolerate for very long without some defensive reaction to it. Thus, the fear is translated into anger. This anger may be externally directed at other people, at abstract ideas ("What lousy luck!"), or at the affected part(s) of the body. Anger directed at the affected parts of the body usually results in denial of their existence or ownership by the stroke patient. However, such denial may also be the result of organic brain damage. Therefore, a hasty evaluation of denial as an expression of anger would be inappropriate. Internally directed anger usually manifests itself in depression. Other signs of depression are lack of motivation, inattention, and confusion (Daylong, pp. 122, 126).

Besides these emotional reactions, there are intellectual reactions caused by brain damage. First, there are the perceptual disturbances which are "difficulties in organizing environmental stimuli of both psychological and physical origin. Responses become hesitant, stereotyped, fragmented, and ineffective. When given a task requiring the organization of material derived from sensory stimuli, the patient may complain of his inability to solve the problem" (Sahs and others, p. 215).

Second, there are thinking disturbances, which are characterized by failures of abstraction and include the following: "inability to account for thoughts and actions; tendency to shift from one aspect of a situation to another; failure to keep in mind all aspects of a task or to grasp the esentials of a problem as a whole; failure to consider the future, focusing attention instead on the immediate present; withdrawal from reality; inability to grasp conceptual symbols or to identify common properties in diverse settings" (Sahs and others, p. 215). Helping the patient and his family to come to terms with these disabilities and reactions requires superb skill and patience on the part of the pastor.

GUILT, HOSTILITY, REJECTION, AND GRIEF

The pastor should remember a basic principle in helping the stroke patient deal with guilt, hostility, rejection, and grief: before positive feelings can come in, negative feelings must be aired out. However, the proper expression and sharing of these feelings can only take place within a supportive and trusting relationship and in an atmosphere of security, acceptance, and understanding. The pastor who is not judgmental but is able to accept the patient unconditionally—that is, without any conditions attached to the acceptance—can be very effective in providing such a therapeutic environment.

The symbolic role of the pastor not only makes it easier for the patient to confide some disturbing thoughts and feelings, but also helps him deal with them. For example, the feelings of hostility and guilt have theological overtones. The patient may be feeling guilty, thinking that the stroke is God's punishment for his sins. Or, he may be feeling angry and hostile toward God for the misfortune, and also be feeling guilty for having such feelings. In counseling, these feelings are likely to be projected to the pastor through the process of transference because of the One he represents. The manner in which the pastor deals with this transference is crucial to the resolution of the patient's negative feelings. If the pastor can accept and respond appropriately to this hostility or anger toward himself, he is able to help the patient accept his misfortune and be reassured of God's acceptance of him regardless of his stroke.

From time to time the feeling of hostility or anger may be expressed, especially by the aphasic, using swearing and cursing. A pastor who is not accustomed to such language may likely feel uncomfortable and overreact under such circumstances. What the pastor should understand is that there are different modes of expressing hostility or anger, which vary with individual patients and are determined by the environment in which they were brought up. Often the only mode of expressing his feeling of hostility or anger the patient knows is swearing and cursing. He may use the same mode to express grief.

The therapeutic relationship of understanding and acceptance can also help the patient deal with his grief. This is so-called "grief work" and its chief goal is the internal process of gradual emancipation from the loss of body function and loss of independence which results from it. The pastor initiates this process by directly, but gradually, helping the patient to recognize and accept the extent of his residual disability. In the context of a continuing supportive relationship the patient will accept the loss, grieve adequately, and recover emotional equilibrium.

The importance of confronting the patient with the knowledge of his disability early in his treatment was demonstrated in a study done by Shapiro and McMahon. This study indicated that when patients were directly confronted with the extent of their disabilities early in their treatment, they were initially upset but then began to work toward an acceptance of the disability. The study also showed that excessive and false assurance served only to reinforce denial and dependence (Shapiro and McMahon, pp. 173-177). It is important for the pastor to help the patient accept himself realistically and fully so that he can concentrate all his capabilities on participating in his prescribed treatment.

EMPATHY

In any counseling or therapeutic situation a good rapport must be established from the outset if positive results are to be expected. Establishing a good rapport means to find, and to be, where the patient is in the here-and-now.

In counseling, the emphasis on the state of being is not so much on what the counselee is thinking about as on what he is feeling. In other words, the counselor is more interested in where the counselee is on the affective (feeling) or "gut" level at the particular moment of face-to-face encounter than on the cognitive (thinking) or "cerebral" level.

The reason for this stance is based on the belief that intellectualizing presents a front, or veneer, which covers up the feelings. The feelings actually are the real indication of where the counselee is at that moment. The analogy to remember is that the most direct route from one point to another is a straight line. Likewise, in counseling the most direct route to the heart of the counselee is the straight line the counselor takes on the affective level.

It is through empathy that the counselor enters into the affective level of counseling interaction. This is the counselor's best tool, enabling him to make connections between his world and the counselee's world.

Empathy is "the process whereby one individual comes to understand the feelings and experiences of another (person) in the here-and-now of a face-to-face encounter, and successfully communicates this understanding to the individual" (Stetler). From the counselee's standpoint, empathy may be defined as his "perception of being understood by the counselor" (Wagenfeld).

Knowledge of the patient's background is necessary for the pastor to be able to empathize with the stroke patient. Particularly, knowledge of the patient's mental and physical deficits as determined by diagnostic evaluation is important in understanding his feelings and experiences as the result of stroke. Therefore, the pastor should acquaint himself with as much information about the patient as possible before he initiates pastoral counseling with him. The pastor obtains this knowledge by talking to the physician, other members of the treatment team, and relatives, and by reviewing the patient's medical charts.

Having empathy for the stroke patient in counseling also requires an understanding appropriate to what the patient is feeling and experiencing at the particular moment. The patient usually thinks his feelings and experiences are unique to himself. Their uniqueness should be recognized and should never be minimized by generalization for the sake of conveying understanding and sympathy. For this reason it is not necessarily true that a person who has experienced a stroke himself has more empathy for the stroke patient. On the contrary, such a person may be prone to generalize his own experiences to the patient's experiences, and thus fail to understand what the patient is experiencing at the particular moment.

For understanding and empathy to have therapeutic value, they must be communicated during the face-to-face encounter. Delayed or subsequent communication of the understanding will lose its effectiveness no matter how accurate the understanding might have been.

In a counseling situation the pastor can have and show real empathy by responding to the feeling tone, or the undertone, of what has been expressed rather than to the literal sense of the words. The pastor also functions as a mirror by reflecting back to the patient his expressed feelings. The patient expresses himself in gestures, crying, laughing, facial expression, writing, etc., in addition to his modified speech. Usually it takes the utterances of more than one or two sentences on the part of the patient before the pastor is able to pick up the patient's feeling tone. Hence, the pastor should be careful not to cut off the patient's trend of thoughts by interrupting. The pauses of silence are likely to tempt the pastor to interrupt because they may be difficult to tolerate. However, if the pastor too can remain silent, he will often discover that his silence will encourage the patient to go on to complete what he had started to express.

One of the ways the pastor may interrupt the patient's expression of feelings is by excessive questioning for information. The presence of less empathy may be assumed whenever the interaction between the pastor and patient takes the form of question-and-answer. The study by Stetler indicates that the least empathetic counselors were found to seek significantly more information from the patients than did their high empathy counterparts.

It appears that if the pastor is aware of and accepts what is taking place within himself under anxiety-provoking counseling situations, he will be able to tolerate silence and will be less interruptive by excessive questioning. It also appears that a pastor who has developed an optimum self-awareness has more empathy for his patient because his self-knowledge enables him to understand the patient. This has been demonstrated in Wegenfeld's study, which affirmed a significant relationship between the counselor's self-awareness and his empathy with the patient.

RELIGIOUS RESOURCES

In counseling stroke patients a pastor may include religious resources such as prayer, scripture, and devotional literature. Clinebell suggests the use of these resources as one of the methods for supportive counseling (pp. 143, 144). The intrinsic value of these resources in bringing comfort, strength, and renewal experience to patients has been well demonstrated. However, their effective use depends a great deal on knowing when and how they are best presented.

In order to use these resources effectively the pastor must first prepare the heart of the patient so that he will accept this spiritual input. This laying of groundwork is essential because the pastor will not necessarily find all patients in the right frame of mind, oriented toward and ready for spiritual matters. They may be preoccupied with disturbing emotional reactions, as described previously.

The success of counseling with stroke patients depends on how the pastor capitalizes on the emotional state of the patient at the outset. The pastor must consider the patient's emotional state as a point of contact or an entry into the phenomenological world of the patient. Once the pastor enters the patient's world he is able to perceive reality as the patient perceives it. This enables him to empathize and feel with the patient. As he reflects these feelings back to the patient it reassures the patient that the pastor understands him. When the patient reaches this point in the counseling process he is ready for spiritual input. In fact, it has been the author's experience with stroke patients that when the pastor lays down such groundwork the patient takes the initiative in making spiritual input during counseling sessions.

All of this helps the pastor to understand the patient's needs, and thus to select the religious resources relevant to the patient. Oates expressed something in this line of thought when he stated that the pastoral counselor must have some "feeling entrée" into the context of the parishioner's life if Scripture interpretation is to be adequate (p. 72). Of course, this principle also applies to the presentation of prayer and devotional materials.

Thus, the effective use of these religious resources is determined by their relevance to the patient's needs. However, the pastor should always be aware of the possibility of misusing these religious resources. For example, he may use them to avoid meaningful human contacts with stroke patients. He may do this unconsciously to compensate for his own feelings of inadequacy, discomfort, or anxiety in counseling situations.

Therefore, it is important for the pastor to recognize these feelings and use them to develop increased counseling skills. This will give him greater confidence in his own strengths and inner resources. In addition, it will help him derive greater satisfaction from a meaningful relationship and helping interaction with the patient.

INTERMEDIATE AND LONG-TERM GOALS

The goals of counseling the stroke patient must address themselves to three basic human needs if they are to contribute to the rehabilitation of these patients. These three basic human needs are, namely, the need for relatedness, the need for independence, and the need for self-esteem. The need for relatedness is satisfied in human relationships by living and being loved. This need for relatedness sometimes conflicts with the need for independence, but these two needs are in harmony in mature individuals. A person achieves independence through two distinct phases of human development. The first is the process of individuation in infancy by which he becomes physically independent from the symbiotic mother-child relationship. The second phase comes in adolescence when a person becomes psychologically independent from the advice and support of the parents. Subsequently, he continues to grow in self-sufficiency and self-determination, thus fulfilling his need for independence.

The person whose needs for relatedness and independence are met has self-esteem, which enables him to fulfill certain roles in life and to make contributions to society. In this manner, his need for self-esteem is fulfilled. Insofar as these basic needs are closely related to each other, each basic need requires the satisfaction of the other needs for its fulfillment.

Why is stroke so devastating to the victim? It is because it cripples the person's abilities to fulfill these basic needs. For example, stroke reduces a person to an existence of physical and often psychological dependence in some degree. This dependence lowers the stroke patient's self-esteem, and in turn diminishes his ability to relate to others in a need-satisfying manner.

The total rehabilitation program helps the stroke patient to recover from his disability. Pastoral counseling concentrates on not only providing support during the process of rehabilitation, but helps these patients meet their basic needs of relatedness, independence, and self-esteem.

CRITERIA FOR EVALUATION

There are five criteria suggested by Clinebell for evaluating the success of pastoral counseling (p. 20). In adapting these criteria to evaluate the success of counseling stroke patients, the author has restated each criterion in several ways.

1. "How well does the counseling help persons to handle their load of problems and responsibilities?"

   a. Has the counseling helped the stroke patients in their efforts to overcome their problems rather than passively accept them?

   b. Has the counseling helped the stroke patients to become amenable to accepting available assistance in order to cope with their problems?

c. Has the counseling helped the stroke patients to accept their new role as members of their families and
the responsibilities which this entails?

2. "How well does the counseling help persons to continue to
grow toward the fulfillment of their unique personhood?"

a. Has the counseling helped the stroke patients to grow
in their ability to give and receive love?

b. Has the counseling helped to release the trapped
potentialities and creativity of stroke patients caused
by a traumatic crisis in their lives?

c. Has the counseling helped stroke patients to grow in
awareness, sensitivity, and self-acceptance?

3. "How well does the counseling help persons to develop
constructive relationships?"

a. Has the counseling helped stroke patients to accept
their disabilities and the resultant emotional reactions so that complexes, defensiveness, or self-pity
will not interfere with their ability to relate with
people?

b. Has the counseling helped stroke patients to participate in a relationship characterized by mutual
sensitivity and responsiveness to the needs of others?

c. Has the counseling helped stroke patients reduce the
inner blocks which prevent them from relating in
need-satisfying ways?

4. "How well does the counseling help the stroke patients'
relationship with God to become increasingly meaningful?"

a. Has the counseling helped stroke patients to have a
true concept of a God who is love?

b. Has the counseling helped stroke patients in their
misfortune to see, not a punishing God, but a mer-
ciful God who loves them regardless of their
disabilities?

c. Has the counseling helped stroke patients to develop
a loving, trusting relationship with God?

5. "How well does the counseling help the person to become
a renewal agent in his family, community, and church?"

a. Has the counseling helped stroke patients to extend their lives beyond the locked walls of their physical disabilities toward a more abundant and independent life, thus becoming whole and productive persons in society?

b. Has the counseling helped stroke patients to find that niche in life where they can still be contributing and productive members in the family, community, and church?

c. Has the counseling helped stroke patients to become instruments for deepening relationships by discovering new life in their own depths?

Ideally, a pastor who has been fully successful in helping stroke patients by providing effective pastoral counseling will fulfill all of the above criteria.

BIBLIOGRAPHY

Anderson, Thomas P., and others. "Predictive Factors in Stroke Rehabilitation." *Archives of Physical Medicine and Rehabilitation* LV:12 (1972): 544-553.

Aspy, David N. "Helping Teachers Discover Empathy." *Humanist Educator* XIV:2 (1975):56-63.

Bell, D. S. "Psychiatric Aspects of Cerebral Vascular Disease." *The Medical Journal of Australia*, October 29, 1966, pp. 829-833.

Charatan, Frederich B., and Albert Fisk. "Mental and Emotional Results of Strokes." *New York State Journal of Medicine* LXXVIII:8 (1978):1403-1405.

Clinebell, Howard J., Jr. *Basic Types of Pastoral Counseling*. New York: Abingdon Press, 1866.

Daylong, William B. "Beyond the Wall of Silence: Pastoral Care of the Stroke Patient." *Journal of Pastoral Care* XXVIII:2 (1974):122-123.

Feigenson, Joel S., and Mary L. McCarthy. "Guidelines for Establishing a Stroke Rehabilitation Unit." *New York State Journal of Medicine* LXXVII:9 (1977):1430-1434.

Fields, William S., and William A. Spencer. *Stroke Rehabilitation*. St. Louis: Warren H. Green, Inc., 1967.

Fine, Virginia K., and Mark E. Therrien. "Empathy in the Doctor-Patient Relationship: Skill Training for Medical Students." *Journal of Medical Education* LII:9 (1977):752-757.

Fowler, Roy S., Jr., and W. E. Fordyce. *Stroke: Why Do They Behave That Way?* Washington State Heart Association, 1974.

Hyman, Martin D. "Social Psychological Determinants of Patients' Performance in Stroke Rehabilitation." *Archives of Physical Medicine and Rehabilitation* LII:5 (1972):217-226.

Jones, F. Haven. "Rehabilitation of the Stroke Patient." *American Family Physician* XV:1 (1977):178-182.

Marshall, John. *The Management of Cerebrovascular Disease.* Boston: Little, Brown & Company, 1968.

Oates, Wayne E. *The Bible in Pastoral Care.* Philadelphia: Westminster Press, 1953.

Oradei, Donna M., and Nancy S. Waite. "Group Psychotherapy with Stroke Patients During the Immediate Recovery Phase." *American Journal of Orthopsychiatry* XLIV:3 (1974):386-395.

Page, Irvine H., and others. *Strokes.* New York: E. P. Dutton & Co., Inc., 1961.

Patterson, C. H. *Theories of Counseling and Psychotherapy.* New York: Harper & Row, Publishers, 1966.

Rigoni, Herbert C. "Psychologic Consideration in Evaluating and Treating the Stroke Patient." *Clinical Orthopaedics and Related Research* LXIII (March-April 1969):94-101.

Sahs, A. L., and others. *Guidelines for Stroke Care.* Bureau of Health Planning and Resources, Health Resources Administration, Public Health Service, Department of Health, Education, and Welfare, 1976.

Shapiro, Leon N., and Arthur W. McMahon. "Rehabilitation Stalemate." *Archives of General Psychiatry* XV (August 1966):173-177.

Smith, Genevieve. *Care of the Patient with a Stroke.* New York: Springer Publishing Company, 1976.

Stern, Peter Hans, and others. "Factors Influencing Stroke Rehabilitation." *Stroke* IL:3 (1971):213-218.

Stetler, Cheryl B. "Empathy, Communication and Related Variables Among Registered Nurses." Unpublished doctoral dissertation, University of Kansas, 1977.

Struss, Alma B., and others. "Groupwork with Stroke Patients." *Rehabilitation Record* VIII:6 (1967):30-32.

Ullman, Montague. *Behavioral Changes in Patients Following Strokes.* Springfield, Ill.: Charles C. Thomas, 1962.

Wagenfeld, Jeanne. "A Psychological Investigation of the Relationship of Empathy, Self-Awareness and Telepathy in the Counselor-Client Dyad." Unpublished doctoral dissertation, Western Michigan University, 1977.

R. H. Ferris

4

Pastoring the Family
of the Institutionalized

THE PROBLEM

Will and Joyce have had a "rollercoaster" marriage. Will's ego is fragile and he maintains an aggressive "front" to protect it. Joyce is very dependent on Will but resists his control. Her first pregnancy settled things a bit but the first child, a girl, is a classic Down's syndrome (mongoloid). Immediate relational tension surfaced. A second child, a male, was also afflicted, but to a lesser degree. You are called upon for help in making a decision between institutionalizing the children or continued home care when the children are eight and eleven years of age.

Mary is a rather rebellious fifteen-year-old daughter of a very traditional and conservative couple and was born when the parents were in their late thirties. Mary has had no steady social life yet, but became pregnant. Mary insists she will keep the child. Her parents refuse to support her financially but are unable to accept her dependence on welfare support in order to raise the child. You are asked to help resolve the issue in your pastoral role.

Henry is hospitalized for the third time following surgery that has been unsuccessful in arresting malignancy. The doctor has told Henry's wife that death is imminent. All their married life Henry and his wife have been committed Christians, "health-conscious", and carefully selected their diet, vitamin supplements, and life style. You are called by the wife, who is totally unable to accept the fact of cancer and the prospect of Henry's death in view of their careful lifestyle.

John has been the family "darling" who could do no wrong. He has been able to attain recognition and realize a degree of success in varied enterprises. You receive a phone call from a relative who confides that John is in the county jail on a charge of child molestation. The relative wants you to "straighten John out" and get the "foolish" charge dropped.

Margaret is one of two girls and two boys in a family. All are very close to the parents and each other. Mother and father are now in their nineties and Margaret has taken them into her home. The mother is becoming very senile and cannot be left unattended. Father is enamored with a new wood stove that resembles heating units used on the old homestead. He changes damper settings continually and has caused dangerous overheating of the stove. Margaret, near nervous collapse, insists on continuing to care for them in her home. Her sister and brothers suggest a nursing home and, for Margaret's benefit, they finally insist. Shortly after institutionalizing them the mother dies. Father continually insists on returning to Margaret's home. Margaret visits him several times a day and on occasion interferes with the nursing home staff concerning her father's care. The brothers and sister ask you to sit down with the family and help them work through the problem.

David is a twelve-year-old retarded child who was placed in a state school when he was six and is unable to attend a regular school program. He has been trained to the degree of being able to take care of his own basic personal hygiene. The state is in the process of "de-institutionalizing" and has told David's parents they must assume responsibility for his care. David is an only child and after institutionalization his parents immersed themselves in careers where they have attained notable success. They never talked about or visited David. Few of their associates are aware of David. You are asked by the state school to assist the parents in accepting David and providing for his care.

In each of these brief case histories you are given a problem calling for a counselor. How would you respond? What elements are common to all cases, what elements are unique? What counseling principles apply? Keep these questions and the context of the case histories in mind as the issues facing the families of the institutionalized and those who work with them are analyzed in this chapter.

TYPES OF INSTITUTIONALIZATION

A century ago most people were cared for by their families in the home environment unless they were judged to be mentally incompetent or criminal. The industrialization of society and the urbanization of its population around industrial centers has eroded the family social structure that offered such care. Governmental concern for disadvantaged citizens has largely transferred care formerly provided by the extended family to institutions created and supported by the government. Renewed concern about individual human dignity and "rights" is beginning to draw the problem full circle.

Four general categories broadly include most institutionalized persons. They are physical incapacitation, social deviance, military personnel, and the bureaucratically institutionalized.

The physically incapacitated are dependent on others for all or part of their care. For example, the hospitalized include accident victims, those with physiological crises, those receiving elective therapies, those being supervised in normal processes like childbirth, those receiving post-crisis rehabilitative treatment, and the terminally ill. With the exception of the terminal patient, most will be institutionalized for relatively short periods with a somewhat predictable discharge point.

Also included in the classification of physical incapacitation are those with psychological malfunctions. The acute depressive reaction, the manic that poses a threat to others, and the suicidal are some examples. The alcoholic and drug dependent may be included when they are not in an acute, immediate crisis.

Longer term physical incapacitation may find people institutionalized in retirement centers, enriched housing, and nursing homes. Custodial care for physical incapacitation is provided in institutional settings for the congenitally deformed such as the hydrocephalic, the cerebral palsied, epileptic, the severely retarded, and the physically handicapped para- and quadriplegic.

A new trend toward homebound family care is presently developing. It might be argued that such care is not institutionalized, but, in the opinion of this writer, many of the same stigmata and problems are present in the dynamics of family interaction in homebound and specialized care settings as are in the formalized institutional setting.

Institutionalized social deviants are those jailed or free on bond awaiting indictment and trial, those incarcerated after being judged guilty and receiving a sentence, probationers, parolees, and juveniles under jurisdiction of juvenile or family courts. The incarcerated include those with short-term sentences in local facilities, those with long-term sentences (often in correctional facilities remote from family and friends), and those with indeterminate sentences such as the criminally insane confined in state mental hospitals.

The pastor faces most of these problems in the course of his career. Often the process of having to face such experiences is the only training he gets to make more positive responses in future counseling. This is a hard and often uncomfortable way to learn to cope with some very frustrating problems.

COMMON DENOMINATORS

Think back to our case illustrations. Are there recognizable common threads in all or most of them? If the pastoral counselor can find common elements and prepare a methodology for constructively dealing with them, future cases will pose less of a personal and professional threat while providing more opportunity to render positive, growth-inducing help.

Probably one omnipresent factor is a sense of helplessness growing out of an unavoidable situation. Because I am a family member, we think to ourselves, what happens to all other members of the family impacts upon me. Since I am in an ongoing process of self-evaluation, my self-image is assaulted; therefore, I must struggle until personal equilibrium is restored.

Will, in our first illustration, had to deal with his macho self-image when he had fathered one mongoloid child. Since it was a girl he could easily assume the defect was attributable to Joyce's genes. Then a second mongoloid child was born—a son! Can you picture his feelings of helplessness? Joyce loved her daughter and assumed that she was one of those infrequent cases where genes went wrong; but when her son also was abnormal, how could she really believe she was a normal person? Extend this to the feelings of all four grandparents, who did not really approve of the marriage in the first place but were helpless to prevent it.

Mary felt helpless once her pregnancy was confirmed. Her parents felt panic, compounded with helplessness by finding themselves trapped and bound at the same time by their lack of control over Mary. Their moral convictions about abortion are an impediment. They are too old to raise the child themselves or continue to provide a home for three generations. All of these problems must be worked through. Besides, what will the neighbors, the church, their friends, and their business associates think?

Henry was helpless to combat his disease. His wife questioned where she had "gone wrong" in planning Henry's diet. Nothing that could be done in the present could change the insidious advance of the disease. Helplessly, she stood by as the institutions of modern medicine mechanically cared for Henry and she awaited the inevitable death of her companion. Her only outlet was the constant verbalization of "what if I only had . . . " statements to friends and family.

John is diagnosed by the court psychiatrist and labeled "gay". His family is encouraged to accept him and his homosexuality, yet they feel that morally this cannot be the correct approach. As the newspaper publishes the progress of the court case the family is helpless and withdraws from the community for fear of criticism, ridicule, and loss of face.

Margaret loves her parents. She feels impelled to care for them at home even if it costs her physical and emotional health; she struggles to maintain her drive to "help" her father. When finally confronted by family and nursing home staff she is compelled to give in. What happens within her, though, as her guilt compounds?

David's parents have avoided their helplessness by transferring their parental feelings to a career. For a period of years they built a life style comfortable for them. Suddenly there is a new confrontation—and equally helpless feelings. Must they bring David home? How can they care for him? The financial costs? What will David's existence and presence do to their carefully developed community image?

Helplessness and its implications for self-image make up the first universal factor that the counselor must deal with. Later we shall discuss methods that can be used to reduce this primary problem in the families of the institutionalized.

Anger runs a close second to helplessness as a common denominator. Anger is often first directed toward the diagnostician, then toward the institution. Ultimately, self, God, and even the problem individual himself are drawn within the aura of anger one feels.

The counselor must be sensitive for indirect manifestations of anger. Will constantly yelled and argued with Joyce. Joyce refused to talk with Will's parents. Will quit a secure profession and went into a series of risky and non-productive business ventures. Mary told her parents she got pregnant because she didn't think parents as old as they were could love a teenage child. She needed to be loved even if she had to create a "lovee" with her own body. Henry and his wife blamed God but then felt immediate and intense guilt. Failing to resolve their anger in this way, they next attacked the doctors for failing to diagnose earlier, technicians for inappropriate or delayed tests and therapy. For a time a malpractice suit was even considered. John was angry with the boy who went to the police when sexually propositioned. That anger grew to include the police, the prosecutor, his lawyer, the judge. It was only after John had directed anger toward his family, who had always praised his every action as a boy, that he could begin to co-operate with the institutions that sought to correct and help him. John's family members also had to be helped in working through their anger with him for acting in such an anti-social way, according to their standards.

How do you think anger was evident and acted out in Margaret's case? What anger would David's parents experience toward him and the authorities who "resurrected" their painful past and thrust it on them as a new and unavoidable responsibility?

Helplessness, assault on one's self-image, and anger are common to the institutionalized person, each family member, and the family structure. Externally, anger may be presented as a response to being deprived of "normal" social contact, but deeper examination demonstrates it to be a response to the erosion of self-image exacerbated by the helplessness that is present.

Yet another common denominator is frustration. What could Will and Joyce do? They attempted to read and learn all they could about training (curing?) mongoloids. Despite their effort and best intentions, neither child responded to a significant degree. They poured out all the love they were capable of but no response came from the children. Could they express their frustration to the children? Of course not. So they expressed it in their relations to each other!

A key factor in frustration is the open-ended prospects for resolution. At a time when the family most intensely attempts to deal in specifics, there is the greatest need to approach the issues more broadly. When one specific response is desired, the ability to examine other options becomes restricted and, in fact, further feeds the sense of frustration. Mary's parents knew they couldn't control her behavior so the only option for them was abortion and possible sterilization to prevent future control of their lives by Mary. They became intensely frustrated and angry because Mary saw other options. Mary was in an ideal position to manipulate her parents as an expression of her frustration and anger toward them. In this perverse retaliatory sort of way she could build a sense of self-esteem. This type of circular behavior must be identified by the counselor before remedial intervention is possible or he only joins the "game" as just another player in the circle.

Pastoral counselors dealing with parishioner clients will nearly always find guilt as an integral factor in counseling families of institutionalized and handicapped persons. Guilt in these situations is of three types. There is corporate guilt simply because of membership in the family, a sort of "genetic guilt". There is guilt by association: "Since he is, therefore, I must be, too." There is also guilt by implication: "Since there is a family problem, I must have contributed to it." Cast in a context of the spiritual community, the religious person also adds divine implications, converting a pre-sin guilt to sin itself. This is the problem presented to Jesus in John 9:2 when the disciples asked concerning the blind man, "Who sinned, this man or his parents?" Henry and his wife experienced guilt by implication, having failed to deal as Christians with their own mortality.

While generalized anxiety is a factor present in all counseling with families of the institutionalized, anxiety concerning alternatives is acute. As frustration self-limits the consideration of options, anxiety often leads family members to blame the present problems on some vague spiritual failure. This type of anxiety prevents the appropriation of previously-developed faith to help in the present situation. Anxiety is seen in many phrasings of the basic question, "Have I made all of the right choices?" The counselor needs to help the family rephrase the question to, "Have I made the *best* choices?" in reducing anxiety levels.

The tendency to run from the issue, or the "bury-the-head-in-the-sand" response, is another common denominator. David's parents had done this when they committed him to the state at six years of age. They chose to ignore the issue, deny their own feelings about both David and themselves, and disclaim all responsibility from that point on. At best, this is only a temporary solution. Good mental and spiritual health demands a working through of the sense of helplessness, anger, frustration, and anxiety of the family faced with an institutionalized family member.

The last common factor to be considered here is seen as a result of the others. Growth as persons in all dimensions of life requires an openness to God, self, and others. The factors mentioned as common denominators all tend to block personal growth. Blockage occurs through preoccupation with problems, by the sheer mass of obstacles to be surmounted, by draining of psychic and spiritual energy, and by replacing natural optimism with a crippling pessimism. Fortunately, when the causes are worked through, this problem of personal growth often largely cares for itself.

THE COUNSELOR

It is not facetious to say, "A counselor is a counselor is a counselor." Qualities of a good counselor of families of the handicapped and institutionalized do not markedly differ from those of a good pastoral or psychiatric counselor. The difference occurs in an awareness of how the situation being approached incorporates basic behavioral responses. Sensitized to these dynamics, the counselor can effectively become a helping person. Let's review some of these universal qualities.

The basic ingredient of an effective counselor of families with institutionalized members is perceptive listening. Being a good listener as the clients verbalize their concerns and questions means avoiding quick answers that will negate the healing "process" so vital in coping with the helplessness, frustration, anger, and blocked personal growth. The counselor must carefully perceive many "hidden agendas" that are only alluded to or avoided because of pain or a simple lack of awareness. Often metacommunication (an unspoken message sent as part of a spoken one) must be recognized and identified by the counselor-listener.

Counselor qualities of empathy, non-judgmental objectivity, supportiveness, and acceptance are crucial. Accepting what the client verbalizes as being, in fact, reality for him is a key skill. Only then can the focus of the counseling process move to the resolution of issues.

Perhaps no other area of counseling demands more creativity in establishing options than counseling families of the institutionalized. A marriage counselor need not be divorced to counsel divorced or divorcing persons. It helps that most counselors are family members. Creativity demands that we move beyond our own family experiences in order to adequately assist in the discovery of options. Leading the clients to choose among options also calls for creativity and patience.

Peacock (1979) has observed, "A person's fears and anxieties become more intense when there is not an understanding and accepting person around." Pastoral counselors may find it difficult to be both understanding and accepting. A distinction exists between accepting what we understand has been said and agreeing with it. Since pastors teach God's absolute will, they may be less accepting of other viewpoints, believing that acceptance is necessarily equated with agreement. You may not agree with John's homosexuality, but you must understand it before help can be given.

Noted counselor Carl Rogers hypothesized three significant factors found in successful psychotherapy regardless of the therapist's "school of thought" or training. They are: (1) congruence, (2) accurate empathy, and (3) unconditional positive regard (Truax and Charkoff, 1976). Congruence implies that the behavior and intentions of the counselor match his actions, both verbally and non-verbally. Accurate empathy is perceptively understanding (not necessarily agreeing with) the stated disclosures and emotional responses of the client. Unconditional positive regard declares to the client that he is valued by the counselor where he is now in his personal growth. Such counselors provide an atmosphere of trust that facilitates the disclosure and acceptance of feelings leading to the experiencing of hope and the resolution or reduction of anxiety.

Welter suggests that the counselor must see people responding on four distinct channels: feeling, thinking, choosing, and doing (1979). When dissonance exists between thinking and feeling, anxiety is produced. Thinking is a rational process; feeling is an emotional process. Thinking is what I should do. Feeling is what I emotionally want to do. In helping the families of institutionalized persons, this distinction is at the root of understanding their anxiety.

Choosing a course of action and failing to carry it out also creates dissonance. The counselor must carefully avoid stopping after choices have been made or he abets increased anxiety. The counselor must assist in implementation of choice as well.

The counselor, as a person, seeks to tune in on how both he/she and the client handle the issues at hand on all four of Welter's levels if they are to work on the problem together and facilitate growth. Here the wisdom of David and Vera Mace, the founders of the Association of Couples for Marriage Enrichment, bears mention in distinguishing between group leaders and facilitators. A leader is technically proficient and directs the process of growth. A facilitator, on the other hand, is technically proficient and participates in the growth experience. While the implications of this distinction may not seem to be all that important at first glance, consider some applied contrasts.

The leader classifies information and extends it through interpretation to the group or individual. He seeks a diagnosis in order to prescribe a treatment for others.

The facilitator does not presume to know how the client feels—instead he attempts to feel with him. He is not intent on diagnosis or clarification. He frankly admits he does not have answers but sets out to find them with the client. He creates an atmosphere for joint exploration of all dimensions in the present situation. He calls on individual and family strengths, on spiritual resources of the family, and openly shares of himself. The facilitator assumes a mutual learning goal. He makes referrals when they are deemed to be helpful in reaching mutual learning goals.

Helping people in crisis is a team effort but the facilitator sees the team as people with a joint goal, not separate specialists each working separately on the same problem. He sees both the client and the professionals involved as team members and active participants. The therapeutic team is growth oriented with the client.

Some counseling basics are mentioned again here because of the vital role they play in facilitating growth. First, "listen much, talk little." Second, interact rather than argue or debate. Third, accept client feelings as genuine and their expression of them as "normal." Fourth, encourage full and free expression of both positive and negative thoughts and feelings about the institutionalized family member.

While much of what has been written in this section so far is applicable to all fields of counseling, mention should be made about the unique position of the pastoral counselor as he helps church families. As a pastor he has six promises to draw on:

(1) The promise of the presence of God with him.
(2) The promise of the perspective of faith.
(3) The promise of the providence of God at work.
(4) The promise of skill as one serving in Christ's stead.
(5) The promise of mutual accountability in a context of spiritual commitment.
(6) The promise to work with the dynamic process of human development that embraces the risks and joys of mutual growth!

(Adapted from C. W. Brister, *The Promise of Counseling*, New York: Harper & Row, 1980, pp. 4, 5).

UNDERLYING FACTORS

Having discussed the problem and the counselor who works with the problem in general, we now shift to some underlying factors. These need to be understood if counseling families of the institutionalized individual is to produce resolution and positive family growth.

1. Any counselor who has experienced the power of family dynamics in even the weakest of family systems readily understands the resistance to institutionalization of any family member, even when the behavior is deviant rather than physiological in origin. Will and Joyce

purchased isolated land and built a home to prevent disturbing their neighbors by their daughter's uncontrollable screams and asocial behavior. Joyce insisted that she would live a hermit existence rather than institutionalize her daughter. She even endured physical assault from the children when they were big and stronger than herself. Henry's wife insisted on home care and "miracle" therapies rather than to see Henry institutionalized in one of the country's leading cancer hospitals. John's maiden sister appeared in court and assumed complete responsibility for her brother in order to prevent his incarceration on sexual molestation and homosexual charges. Margaret intruded into the nursing home and medical care prescribed for her senile father as a "last ditch" attempt to deny the reality of his final institutionalization. David's parents resisted institutionalization for the first six years of his life. When their decision was made, it was complete. They resisted de-institutionalization just as emphatically!

Institutionalization is often seen as a personal admission of failure in coping with the identified problem as a member of the family. Surprisingly strong extended family loyalty exists well into the age of the nuclear family. It provides the motivation for the resistance.

Institutionalization is perceived by most family members as the negative choice-of-last-resort. This mind-set frequently undercuts the ability of institutions to perform growth and healing functions for the affected family member. In fact, this resistance and last resort attitude may be preventing the family member from receiving the help and reaching the very growth and development levels the family declares to be its own objective!

Often resistance to institutionalization has involved a sense of false modesty when it relates to "intimate" medical problems, especially if sexually related. The counselor must be prepared to identify the presence of "last resort" mind-set and false modesty and to facilitate growth towards acceptance of the problem and the acceptance of available institutional help to assist the affected family member.

Within the constraints of modern economic structures, resistance to institutionalization may focus on the loss of a family income producer, the costs of institutional care to the already stressed family, and the thrust toward achieving (or maintaining already achieved) financial and social status. Fortunately, many major employers are now providing extended medical coverages that resolve the issues of economic resistance to institutional care. The one significant area as yet unresolved is dependence on welfare support for the patient. Even families with limited resources resist "abandoning" a family member to bureaucratic institutionalization and dependence on the welfare system for care and support.

2. Another underlying factor is loneliness. The "non-presence" of a family member, no matter how dysfunctional he has been in the family, can cause acute discomfort. Many times the institutionalized family member has, in fact, provided a significant sense of worth to those who support and care for him. His removal leaves a void to be bridged and/or a guilt for not having done more which needs to be resolved.

Loneliness is often aggravated by a restricted or limited opportunity during institutionalization for sexual expression between husband and wife or for role modeling between the developing child and the parents during the process of psychosexual maturation. Visitation of the institutionalized family member, although a necessary part of dealing with guilt, may exacerbate loneliness.

The absence of a family member may precipitate either withdrawal from social contact outside of the family or a clear cutoff of social contact with the institutionalized family member as a means of reducing or containing the discomfort of loneliness. A critical factor includes the insecurity and negative feelings about self that serve to attack the self-esteem of family members. The fear of rejection by friends and other family members because of the institutionalized relative may seriously affect how family members see themselves. In Henry's case, both he and his wife were threatened and anxious because they had failed to come to terms with their own finitude. They saw themselves as less than whole persons because of Henry's terminal illness.

Oddly enough, a weak sense of self-esteem in one family member who has exhibited a lack of great potential for personal growth may actually be enhanced by the institutionalization of another family member. This occurs when a "there, but for the grace of God, go I" attitude is held. Since the patient or deviant is so badly off, it follows that I am perhaps not so bad after all! Such a situation may prevent reception of counseling help, even though requested, unless the counselor detects and deals with it early in the therapeutic program.

3. Uncertainty about the future is an important underlying factor. What limits on future employment will institutionalization place, especially institutionalization for penal or for mental health reasons? While the patient is institutionalized, what will the other partner do about the marriage? Will divorce occur? How can the family or patient plan for their futures as individuals when the duration of institutionalization is uncertain?

4. We have earlier mentioned the role of guilt as an underlying factor. It often is most acute when the family or affected family members are religious persons. Institutionalization may be seen as a test of the validity of personal religious faith. Often attempts at correction of the problems through divine healing or bartering with God through conversion or the promising of life changes may have been seen as unsuccessful. The counselor must carefully probe for such experiences and facilitate an understanding of them on both the intellectual and spiritual levels before acceptance and new growth can occur.

Some well-meaning religious persons ask, "Who sinned?" Like Job's friends, they deduce that if you have a major problem requiring institutional types of attention you indeed must have transgressed against an aggrieved God. This often leads to aggressive self-criticism. "What is 'my contribution' to the defect in the institutionalized family member?" Non-acceptance of personal self-worth and the non-relatedness of most of life's events aren't seen or understood.

Guilt produces a tendency to "cover-up" or deny the reality of the situation. It is theorized that if one ignores it, maybe it will go away, and as it goes away, the guilt will go away, too. The counselor, whether a pastor or a religious lay person, must help the family see that guilt over an institutionalized family member is a product of pretending to be perfect at the same time we are fully aware that we are not.

5. Another significant underlying factor is the problem of facing the reality of institutionalization. There may be a parallel to this experience in the stages through which families and individuals face their own death or that of a loved one. Indeed, dealing with the institutionalization of a loved family member is a form of death—death of the idealized role that family member plays or was to have played in the family.

Thanatologist Elisabeth Kübler-Ross (1969) has developed a model describing five stages through which humans move in dealing with death. The stages are:

(1) denial and isolation,
(2) anger,
(3) bargaining
(4) depression, and
(5) ultimate acceptance.

The birth of a mongoloid child, the announcement of an illegitimate pregnancy, the discovery of homosexuality in a family member, the incarceration for deviant behavior, all inevitably bring an initial denial from members of the family and an attempt to isolate themselves from community scrutiny. Then they may turn on the family member in anger. "Why did you do this? Don't you realize . . . ? Didn't you think? What are the problems? What is my contribution?" Anger surfaces. Then comes the process of bargaining. In the case of Henry and his wife it was almost a pre-bargaining: "If we live right, eat the right things, do the right things, we will be immortal and somehow, God will not let us down." For others, the bargaining continues with the offending family member. "All right, have the abortion, institutionalize the child, take the child back after having institutionalized it, if . . . ", then some qualifier is added. All of this, of course, precipitates the intense anxiety and the deep depression which are often seen.

But ultimately, as with most things in life, the fact of institutionalization must be accepted. The goal of the counselor in dealing with these underlying situations must be to facilitate arrival at the fifth stage of the Kübler-Ross model.

C. S. Lewis probably put it most succinctly when he said, "The frequent attempt to conceal mental pain increases the burden" (1962). Therefore, as the counselor facilitates the family's arrival at Stage Five, many of the other factors are also being dealt with. Perhaps Kübler-Ross's main point is that this is all a process rather than being a simple product that can be seen, grasped, and utilized by the effective family system.

Family members at all levels experience underlying reactions and resistance to the institutionalization of a family member. Children, for example, are concerned about the reaction of their peers when the discovery is made that a family member has been sent to a mental institution, to prison, or perhaps is pregnant or on welfare. For the young child whose parents are the institutionalized family members, growing up with that important circumstance has its own set of problems. It may often lead to behavior that is deviant from socially-accepted norms.

Underlying problems are seen to weave their way through the total experience of the family. Some more obvious events might be categorized as complicating problems.

COMPLICATING PROBLEMS

A family member has been institutionalized for alcoholism. The patient opts to leave before his release is recommended by his therapist.

No contemporary law can hold him institutionalized against his will. How are members of the family to react to this complicating feature? What will David's parents expect of him? They have an impression of what he was like at the time that he was institutionalized and, since they have never visited him, there is a fear of the unknown. What is he like now? Or perhaps John has served his time in prison for child molestation. When he emerges from incarceration, what changes have occurred in him? Has he truly changed? How are other family members to react? How are other smaller children or their parents to react to John? Or Mary: now that her child is born will other men want her? Will they consider her a marriage prospect? How will she take care of the child? She has never been a mother before.

All of these are examples of complicating factors and they require effort on the part of family members to adjust to. It is here that the full range of facilitative counseling sensitivity and skill is called upon.

Therapeutically it is possible that when the family member who has been institutionalized is returned to the family environment, there may be a triggering of past problems in other family members by his very reappearance. Or perhaps, by coming into the home setting, the institutionalized family member may relapse into former behavior patterns, unless adequate preparation has been made by his therapist.

Brister raises an interesting concept which can be labeled the "atonement syndrome". He suggests that institutionalizing may represent not only confinement of individuals for the good of society, but a time of "atonement" or "purification" of all the parties involved. It is a period of suffering in order that they may re-enter a state of innocence (1978, pp. 4, 5).

In dealing with this syndrome a pastoral facilitator/counselor has a unique opportunity. Because of his theological background coupled with counseling skills, he may step in and correct spiritual misconceptions over the presumed process of "suffering as atonement". At the same time he can still allow for a constructive working-through of the real guilt of concerned family members.

STRATEGIES FOR CONSTRUCTIVE COUNSELING

Throughout this chapter we have repeatedly identified underlying assumptions for the main factors. While other chapters will be covering counseling techniques in greater detail, it is important for us to review the underlying assumptions in constructive counseling.

1. The pastoral counselor is not so much a therapist as a caring understander. In this posture he can become a facilitator of growth that develops out of the crisis of institutionalization, perhaps more readily than the purely technical therapist can. This is not to suggest that the technical therapist is to be overlooked or his efforts negated, but rather that the pastoral counselor can fulfill a role that is unique in the process of meeting the needs of families of institutionalized persons.

2. The pastoral counselor, by virtue of his spiritual relations with member families, projects a primary attitude of availability. In the institutionalization process there is a certain remoteness. Often the institution is located some distance from the family residence. The institutional professional staff is often lacking in time to deal with the family and focuses on the "patient". The family sees a "conspiracy of silence" that can only be a bad omen. People often come to pastors freely, maybe more freely at times than pastors would like, because of this attitude of availability. But in the counseling process we are considering here, this is an asset.

3. The personality of the counselor plays an important role as well. "The perceptive counselor (is) . . . one who reaches out under stress with a perception, sensitivity and warmth that is freeing and supportive" (Stewart, 1977). This could not be more true than with the effective facilitator.

4. The pastoral counselor role is essentially a supportive one as family members move toward a self-healing therapy. It allows for the self-maintenance of family equilibrium after an institutionalization experience involving a family member.

5. The pastoral counselor may deal more with processes than with content. Howard W. Stone makes a distinction. "Pastoral care and not just counseling calls for educative counseling through sincere caring" (Clinebell, 1975). Again this is an underlying assumption of what has been suggested in the facilitator's role.

6. Another underlying assumption that perhaps sums up all of the above is that educative counseling or educative facilitating stands in distinct contrast with the pathology model. The family of the institutionalized most often will have no specific pathology. However, no one has ever taught them how to deal with this kind of situation. For that reason, the facilitator role is as much educative as it is therapeutic. In the educative process, knowledge will tend to remove any incipient pathology that has developed as a result of the need to institutionalize a family member.

7. A fundamental strategy for constructive, facilitative, educative counseling is a "counseling contract." Even in an acute crisis,

success possibilities are enhanced by the counseling contract. The counseling contract is defined as mutually stated and accepted ground rules and shared goals for dealing with the problem at hand.

Emphasis must be laid on the fact that it is the mutuality of design and construction of the counseling contract that is the genius of its effectiveness. Many people have great anxiety about seeking counseling help, particularly if they have a strong religious background. Therefore, the counseling contract can embrace the religious faith as a dimension to be considered in all actions and therapy. It can be stated in the contract that an expectant faith in God as healer and as counselor is assumed. The simple statement of this fact may guide and speed the adjustment of the family to the counseling process and therefore hasten the time when they can be completely comfortable.

While most counselors and facilitators will use verbal contracts, there is value in reducing the contract to writing for future reference, particularly if a large number of family members are involved in the counseling process. In this way, each one may be presented with a copy of the contract agreement to be restudied as growth and resolutions are facilitated and roadblocks worked through.

Yet another strategy is to establish goals early. Most counseling of families of institutionalized persons stands in contrast to short-term "crisis counseling". In this strategy, clearly defined shared goals to be achieved through the counseling process are the undergirders of supportive growth. Examples of areas in which goals may be established include reducing guilt, converting the crisis into long-term relational growth beginning points, appropriating personal potential for the benefit of self and the institutionalized family member, promoting movement toward healthy self-awareness, increasing the available repertoire of life skills that move the individuals from a specific crisis context to that of total living, and lastly, a focus on God's ultimate restorative power.

Objectives may be either for the confined or for the non-confined institutionalized family member. It further extends to the reunited family group after institutionalization. A primary objective is the uniting of all family members for the mutual benefit and ultimate long-term growth of the family as a whole and individually.

8. In any strategy for successful family counseling, the element of hope is an essential. Hope stands in stark contrast with anxiety and fear. When anxiety and fear are present, hope seems unrealistic. Without hope, growth cannot occur and effective ministry to the family and the institutionalized member is almost impossible.

Webster defines hope as "desire accompanied by anticipation or expectation." Family counselor Virginia Satir asserts that "hope becomes a new possibility" (1978). "Hope is an essential attitude of the mind which is characterized by mental and emotional openness with its associated physiological corollaries. Without this kind of human openness in living and communication, personal growth is restricted and short-circuited for most of us" (Peacock, 1979). As a strategy, therefore, hope helps the client face fear and anxiety without disowning self or rejecting the situation of institutionalization in his own growth process.

The Christian counselor has a "scene beyond" the present crisis to offer to his client. If it is a terminal illness, if it is an irreparable mongoloid condition, or even if it is an unresolved homosexual problem, the Christian counselor can point to a renewal of perfection in heaven that can aid in dissolving guilt in the present situation.

9. A strategy that is often intuitively used focuses on self-transcending activities, that is, activity which goes beyond the present personal and parochial crisis. All humans have a need to transcend their private worlds and move into a larger sphere. Self-transcending activity is often accomplished by reaching out to help other people who are in the same position. When first diagnosed as prospects for mastectomy, many mastectomy patients are helped by a visit from a woman who has undergone the surgery. Joseph Bailey, in his book *A View from the Hearse* (1969), describes his own helping experience the day his family had buried a son who had died of leukemia. When he returned to thank members of the hospital medical staff for the help and care they had given, the nurse pointed to a woman seated in the waiting room with a young child playing on the floor. He sensed the problem and moved to talk with her. She cut him off. How could he possibly understand what was happening? This was her beautiful child just diagnosed as having leukemia. Joseph Bailey self-transcended his own grief of the moment as he shared his experience with the distraught mother.

There is a crying need in our culture for a public effort to educate people concerning institutionalized disabilities. Much of the agony and pain of families focuses on the fear (or the reality) of a lack of understanding on the part of friends, peers, or the community at large. The family of the chronic alcoholic well benefits from Alcoholics Anonymous and other such self-transcending experiences. Available strategies are, of course, broad and numerous. A facilitator will never overlook the use of referral or support resources. Therefore, to be prepared as a counselor of the families of institutionalized persons, one needs to be conversant with the range of community resources available. Involvement in or creation of small support groups would be a positive step if one has a number of families going through the crisis of institutionalization. The power of group dynamics to free family members from the perceived parameters of their immediate problem to an awareness that others have the same type of problems is an amazing and healing process to observe. It is at this point that the facilitator fades into the background as the internal power of the group takes over to give therapy, support, and healing. The group offers an opportunity for experiential learning and coping within a supportive climate. One might call this active learning in crisis.

10. Many agencies today involve families in the therapeutic approach. In Seattle, the Fred Hutchison Leukemia Therapy approach is worthy of note. There is a constant briefing of family members on the condition and the therapy. The patient and family members participate in record-keeping. They are aware that certain changes in the record indicate crisis. They are clearly told the odds of recovery or extended life span. No false hopes are given, but the family of the institutionalized patient is able to cope better because they are not "in the dark." Creative involvement of family members in the goals and process of treatment or care reduces many of the complicating factors associated with institutionalization.

11. A vital strategy for successful counseling is planning for the return of an institutionalized family member back into the family setting. Timing is critical in this planning. Physical accommodations that may be required need to be worked through well in advance of the return of the individual. In the process of working out these physical accommodation changes, family members become direct participators. Therefore, they will tend to value the institutionalized's return to the normal family environment. There are psychological adjustments and attitudes which need to be worked through. How will we handle visible differences in the family member? How will we handle changed expectations?

12. Lastly, when an institutionalized family member is to be returned to the home, special care must be given to planning methods and means with the family for maintaining the growth of all concerned. It is not sufficient to have the member back and then return to a status quo kind of relationship. Having an institutionalized family member, in fact, may trigger life-long growth patterns in that family's structure.

PITFALLS

No one is perfect. Every facilitator, every counselor, every therapist is ever conscious of the fact that he has made strategic or therapeutic errors in his professional career. An awareness of possible pitfalls can safeguard one from unnecessary errors.

Previously, the counseling contract has been mentioned. Probably a major pitfall is a failure to develop a counseling contract early in the helping relationship.

The failure to deal with one's own attitudes and feelings on issues that lead to or result from institutionalization can interfere with or destroy the helping relationship. A clearly understood personal value system on moral issues such as abortion will help an individual to separate his own feelings from those of the client, with which he may not necessarily agree. The facilitator must be aware, for example, of the problems of colostomy patients. Can he handle the frank discussion of the necessary care? What about penal probation? What about incest? What are the counselor's own values and attitudes? It is essential to avoid the pitfall of projection where personal values are superimposed on the counseled family. The pastoral counselor naturally has a value system that probably is shared in common with the family which has come to him for help. Dogmatic pronouncement is not necessarily understanding, but rather, understanding will hopefully lead us to be open with those whose growth we are attempting to facilitate.

In this same vein, pastoral counselors often tend to do normative counseling. There is a frequent tendency to be judgmental or preachy. It is an easy way which can easily terminate the relationship before the necessary growth and development have occurred. Judgmental and preachy approaches demonstrate a lack of acceptance of the troubled person as a person. They further negate warmth and caring that are so essential for positive growth. Normative counseling tends to deny the problem or to classify it in some pre-determined way. Both of these tendencies inhibit growth.

All counselors are aware of the pitfall of projection in transference. The gratitude response of clients may often be misdirected. The writer recalls visiting a girl who was in a coma. The mother had been a member of the pastor's church at one time. The family requested special prayer for the girl, who had been severely injured in an automobile collision in which she had been at fault. When the girl regained consciousness, continued pastoral visits and prayer created a bond. The individual "fell in love" with the pastoral counselor. Unless the counselor is aware of these feelings of transference very early, they can lead to other problems quite apart from the institutionalization!

In some cases anger will be directed toward the facilitator because of his intrusion into the problem area and continuing unresolved conflict. It is the normal defense mechanism of the family unit at work. The facilitator may be blamed by some family members for much of their problem. Here the "sponge technique" is helpful. If the facilitator is comfortable with himself and with his grasp of the case he is dealing with, he can soak up that hostility in an open way and not deny the expression of anger to the clients. Of course, it is necessary to wring the sponge out in a safe environment. Thank God for counselors' spouses who can accept a lot of these wringing experiences! They are therapists' therapists!

The facilitator must be aware of and willing to accept these situations as they develop without feeding them or cutting them off so abruptly as to alienate and nullify the growth that has occurred to date. Gentleness, yet firmness, is often necessary. But neither are of value without adequate awareness on the part of the facilitator.

Lastly, another pitfall is the lack of familiarity with referral resources. When dealing with religiously-oriented people particularly, one needs to know not only the agency that can help but the general philosophy of that agency, to prepare the clients for what they will meet when they go to that agency for help. There is a need to research in general, but also to research the specific resources available.

REWARDS

Helping and counseling with the families of institutionalized persons, whatever the category of institutionalization that may be involved, is truly pastoral ministry. It is not simply a short-term involvement, but it is an ongoing relationship. In the very ongoing nature of it there is opportunity for the facilitator/counselor's personal growth as a helping person. Over time he actually can become a "personal person" as the problem emphasis decreases and the sense of camaraderie and sharing develops.

In many areas of counseling one works for protracted lengths of time with few, if any, visible results. But in working with the family of the institutionalized, there are visible results as soon as the tension decreases and as all members of the family receive that help which is best for them, in or out of the institutional setting.

Helping Will and Joyce to develop their own sense of self-worth; helping Mary to see the need for putting her child out for adoption and not manipulating her family; helping Henry to accept the reality of his mortality and Henry's wife to realize the future point of reunion at the resurrection; following John for two decades as he wrestles with his own sexual identity; helping Margaret to see that she is a worthwhile, caring person, but that she must allow others to assume their caring roles for her father, too; helping David's family to find a new home for him and to slowly begin to develop a relationship with him as their son; these have all been extremely satisfying experiences.

Oh, yes, there have been tears and strain; there has been puzzlement and, at times, frustration; but in reality it has been an experience of following in the restorative footprints of Christ. What more could any counselor ask!

BIBLIOGRAPHY

Bailey, Joseph. *A View From the Hearse*. Elgin, Ill.: Cook, 1969.

Brister, C. W. *The Promise of Counseling*. New York: Harper & Row, 1979.

Clinebell, H. G. *Growth Counseling for Marriage Enrichment*. Philadelphia: Fortress Press, 1975.

Kübler-Ross, Elisabeth. *On Death and Dying*. New York: Macmillan, 1969.

Lewis, C. S. *The Problem of Pain*. New York: Macmillan, 1962.

Peacock, Edward. "Hope." *Family Life* 39:3 (1979):3.

Satir, Virginia. *Your Many Faces*. Milbray, Calif.: Celectial Arts, 1978.

Stewart, Charles W. "How Effective Are Family Ministries?" *Pastoral Psychology* 25:4 (1977):260-271.

Truax, C. B., and Charkoff, R. R. *Toward Effective Communication in Psychotherapy*. Chicago: Aldine, 1976.

Welter, Paul. *How to Help a Friend*. Wheaton, Ill.: Tyndale House, 1979.

Darold Bigger

5

Group Counseling of the Handicapped

Mary, twenty-eight years old, married, mother of two preschool children, was in an automobile accident and lost the use of her right arm. She lies in the hospital bed, questions spinning in her head. How will she be able to care for her children? They're hard enough to hold onto with both hands! Can she keep her house neat enough to suit her fastidious husband? How will she carry groceries in from the car? Shake hands with guests? Tilt and scrape out the bottom of a pan? Hold a child's head while she washes his hair? Will her husband accept a one-armed hug? Make love to a limp-limbed lady?

Jim has been in a wheelchair for months. He's in his early thirties, has three children and a wife who wants to be a housewife. Just as he passed his C.P.A. exam, he found out he had multiple sclerosis. Paralysis gradually increased and has already affected his star-studded career. He was being groomed for executive management and the first two times someone else was promoted above him, he was angry. Now even he admits his limitations and fluctuates between coping quite well and being in the depths of despair. In addition to his physical deterioration, his moods are creating tension at home and his marriage is in jeopardy.

Jane is twenty-five and physically mature and healthy. She is mentally handicapped, however, and emotionally immature. Her foster parents and she are at odds with each other. She wants to get married and have babies, while her guardians know she is incapable of caring for herself, let alone anyone else.

Tommy is eight and his learning disability is evident enough that he could be placed in a special school. His father is a blue collar worker and refuses to see his son as "stupid." Special education is not allowed, and Tommy is made to attend regular classes where his peers make fun of him and reinforce his failures. At times of self-confidence he passes it off, but more and more often he expresses his hurt by physically lashing out.

In situations like these where there is an individual in apparent need, where does group counseling fit? Would it not be simpler to work with the identified patient in one-to-one contact rather than to diffuse attention and include others? What purpose is there in involving more than one at a time?

It is this type of inquiry to which this chapter addresses itself. One forceful way to underscore the importance of the subject and establish some fundamental justification for group work is to review one of Jesus' healing miracles.

AN EXAMPLE

Jesus was walking along the streets of Jerusalem, disciples clustered around Him. The dust of the streets floated in small, low clouds around their ankles as they talked. Rounding a corner, they came upon a blind beggar sitting on the opposite side of the street.

Engaged in theological thought as they were, the disciples asked a difficult question. It was assumed by many that handicaps were the result of specific sins, and their question reflected the belief. "Who sinned, this man or his parents?"

It was not a trivial issue, a passing comment to keep conversation rolling. It was no idle statement with an assumed response. The challenge of this case was that the man had been blind all his life. So, it was supposed, either he was being punished for something his parents had done or he had committed some prenatal sin.

Those questions had no doubt plagued this man and his family for years. The agony of discouragement and guilt that surely accompanied his handicap were omnipresent in direct expressions like this one by the disciples, or in more subtle insinuations, curious stares of passers-by, avoidance, and rejection. In his agony there was no reason to hope, no promise of improvement. Lifelong despair seemed to be his lot.

Then Jesus came, heard the question the disciples asked, and approached the blind man. The Master confidently asserted that sins were not the cause of this ailment. Quite the opposite: this man's handicap was to become the occasion for a miraculous demonstration of divine healing. Those words of concern may have awakened the nearly extinguished hope of the blind man. Still, no comment on his part is recorded.

Jesus didn't wait to be asked for healing. He began immediately to mix mud, put it on the man's eyes, and tell him to wash it off at the pool of Siloam.

The sensitivity of the Healer to the handicapped had already begun to do its work. Jesus had addressed the alienation, guilt, and anxiety the man experienced. He had been willing to do more than drop a hard coin in an outstretched hand. The blind man had felt compassion, assurance, and acceptance in the tone of voice and gentle touch. His stereotyped position in society as a miserable beggar, isolated from normal human contacts, had been ignored. Jesus met him as a man. He was not condemned or demeaned or manipulated or teased or pitied. He was strengthened with the assurance of his lovableness and challenged with his ability to help himself. So he went to the pool and washed. And saw.

The change in him was as much social and psychological as it was physical. He bounded home through familiar streets he had never seen. Friends and neighbors were incredulous. Seeing those he had known for years but had recognized only by sound and perhaps touch should have elicited from *him* the question, "Are you the one . . . ?" But it was they who asked it. His entire social environment was so caught up in his blindness that once he was no longer blind, they were uncertain if he were himself. To them, he was blind—he was not Joe or Sam or Israel or John. To treat the handicap involved much more than just him. It ultimately included all those who knew him as he once was.

Next to become involved were the Pharisees, incensed because their rules of Sabbath observance had been broken and they wanted to deny the veracity of the miracle. Initially the healed man answered questions simply and directly. His parents were included, and still the questioners were unsatisfied. As the encounter continued, the man's confidence increased until he had turned the tables on his antagonists and put them on the defensive. Rather than admit defeat, they expelled him from their religious communion.

At that moment the Healer, who had been unavailable, reappeared. He came, not to confront those who had attempted to thwart the renewed health of the handicapped, but to affirm the handicapped himself. This despised social reject had expressed an exceptional amount of independent courage by confessing Jesus as a prophet. Perhaps because the social system had only accepted him as a token and used him to demonstrate its own supposed benevolence, he saw more clearly than others that the Pharisees had a great deal to do with his handicap. He saw through their sham and perceived their actual abhorrence of him, and that gave him courage to stand independent of their religious approval. But then, knowing that the healed man was cut off from their human support, Jesus came to offer a replacement, a support system of a different kind, based on the acknowledgment of Him as the Light of the World.

THE HANDICAPPED AS PERSONS

This miracle illustrates several key points in our work with handicapped persons. It demonstrates the need for ambassadors of the Divine Healer to see the handicapped as persons, not as deformities. It is just as inappropriate and destructive to categorize the handicapped by the nature of their disorder rather than the uniqueness of their personhood as it is to do the same thing with fully functioning persons. The kind of healing the handicapped most need from pastors comes as the result of being recognized as individuals with unique characteristics, personality traits, needs, and abilities. Their handicap is only one part of who they are. Each one is an exception to several rules, and we would do well to discover them in this sense rather than as fulfillments of some predetermined category.

THE HANDICAPPED AS PART OF A SOCIAL SYSTEM

The miracle shows how dramatic the impact of handicapped persons is on their social system. To bring them to see themselves in a new light requires that the system be confronted with the change, too. It is very difficult for demoralized handicapped persons to develop a positive view of their lives unless those most directly in contact with them share that attitude shift. Most of Jesus' healing miracles were done in the presence of others, so the crowds could see the change. The handicapped persons could also establish new self-identities by being faced with the new views in which they were held by those around them. Jesus thus demonstrated that it was not just the handicapped who needed healing. Healing was provided for the "well" community, too.

THE HANDICAPPED AND HOPE

The healing of the blind man also illustrates the regenerative power of hope. In this case his hope was tangibly rewarded when the identified handicap was removed. As ministers, we are often faced with the paradox of trying to restore or maintain hope in the face of continued primary symptoms. It would be wonderful if God would miraculously heal everyone. (For a practical discussion of how to cope with life when God's will does not include immediate healing, the reader is referred to Leslie Weatherhead's book, *The Will of God*.) Since that is not true, the focus of hope may not always be the same. (Even in this case the man simply exchanged blindness for the social handicap of excommunication, so he was still left with the need to trust God to help him face life's frustrations.) But the realization that handicaps need not make human life a useless waste is a healing message of relief that many have not heard.

THE HANDICAPPED AND GROUP HEALING

Finally, this miracle is a powerful statement of the strength brought by supportive human fellowship. The confident acceptance of Jesus and the disciples enabled this inadequate social misfit to assertively confront a nation's religious leadership with truth. Seeing himself as others saw him, describing himself to friends first, and experimenting with his new self-image in an accepting environment gave him courage to be himself in the more hostile world.

Most of Jesus' miracles included more than just physical healing. He involved other significant people in the handicapped's life, thus recognizing that to restore one to physical health required more than a private service. The individual needed to be reinstated in human society and the spiritual community, too.

THE CHURCH AS A HEALING COMMUNITY

The church exists as a carrier of healing. It is intended to be a medium through which sick human beings recover by regaining spiritual health, physical vigor, emotional stability, and mental sharpness in a redemptive social climate. To those who are handicapped in any one or several of these ways, the Christian church has a solid foundation for offering help. One is justified in seeking it out as a community of healing persons.

That sentence can be interpreted in two ways. In the first, the church would be comprised of those who are productive in the healing of others. In the second, it would be a group who are themselves being healed. Both are true.

But there is first a primary point of emphasis. The church is a group. It is a part of the human community that has faced itself squarely and found both strengths and weaknesses. While believing that it is connected with God by creation and redemption, it also senses its alienation from Him. That is what elicits the desire for restoration.

The separation from God has become so great that it has also distanced individuals from each other and from themselves. The impact of human isolation may be so severe, in fact, that the initial alienation from God appears to be a secondary state. In cases such as these, human relationships not only reflect the divine-human relationship, but can also greatly hamper its development. So restoring human relationships becomes a necessary step in rebuilding a relationship with God. One author suggests that:

> There are souls perplexed with doubt, burdened with infirmities, weak in faith, and unable to grasp the unseen, but a friend whom they can see, coming to them in Christ's stead, can be a connecting link to fasten their trembling faith upon Christ (White, 1970, p. 297).

The handicapped often fall into that category. They not only face direct physical or mental limitations, but also the emotional and social impact that these limitations bring. Since many secondary responses are the result of contact with others, it is only logical that they be resolved through personal contacts. "By the crowd they have been broken; by the crowd they shall be healed" (Knowles, 1964, p. 16).

For example, the handicapped often feel rejected. Former friends and relatives become tired or frustrated, not knowing how to relate to the handicap on an ongoing basis. Physical accident or disease often makes visible changes that are offensive to others. Physical or mental limitations often exclude the handicapped from participation in activities that are open to others. This repeated, reinforced rejection takes its toll on handicapped persons, who become doubtful about their ability to function in society, sensitive to any hint of exclusion or rejection, suspicious of anyone who appears to like them, unable or unwilling to accept themselves, and ultimately unable to believe that God accepts them either. For such people, loving contact with a healing church can begin to reawaken their confidence in humankind, themselves, and God.

A small church of a few members was located in an isolated farming community. There were no facilities in town nor for miles around for those with either physical or mental handicaps. There was in that same town an overly short, round, disheveled, retarded woman now in her middle years. She had grown up there and was recognized by all as a social misfit. She had, however, been accepted by a local congregation. They recognized her as unique, but precious at the same time. She could not drive a car, so every week a church member picked her up for both midweek meetings and worship services. When the church had social gatherings and church dinners, no one expected her to bring food or participate meaningfully in the discussions that took place, but they did want her to come. The church's attitude was one of acceptance, both of her personhood and her limitations. While seeing her as one whom God loved as much as He loved them, they did not expect her to act or think in the same ways as they. Under the impact of that church's concern, she did not become a withdrawn, drowning, angry, frustrated, mental hospital patient. Because she felt love and acceptance from them, she came to view life in general as an open, exciting experience. And, by the same token, every time the fully functioning members of that congregation saw her, they were able to see how much God's love transforms alienated human beings.

GROUP SUPPORT

Many authors agree that the most perplexing challenge the handicapped face is developing social interaction skills (Empey, 1977, pp. 594-595) and maintaining a healthy self concept in that social interaction (Humes, 1970, p. 164). It is essential for them to find a supportive environment in which they can be acknowledged as important and be accepted as precious. For them, a supportive group is not a luxury but a key element in their attitude toward life. Being exposed either to other handicapped persons or fully functioning individuals who are interested in them can become a significant step on the road to recovery. They need a way to face themselves and society without becoming bitter. They need to know that others with similar difficulties have faced similar challenges. They need to be exposed to the approaches others have used in facing those challenges and coping with life. Knowing someone who has made progress stimulates their growth potential (Colston, 1978, p. 30), and their own self-motivation is enhanced as they contact a caring social community (ibid., p. 25).

The church can become an important agency in personalizing God's love, in expressing divine concern, in motivating self-help, and in facilitating contacts between similarly handicapped persons. Trotzer's outline of the value of groups is particularly applicable here. He described safety, belonging, a sounding board, power, helping and being helped, spectator therapy, feedback for growth, increased counselor contact, and personalized education as advantages of groups (1977, pp. 13-19). All can be effectively used in religious settings. The church as the community of forgiven sinners needs to be a safe sounding board for all who wish to join. It is an environment in which healing persons share their experiences with each other and help enhance mutual healing. Religious organizations provide a base for communicating powerfully to the broader community about the conditions, needs, and assets of the handicapped community. And certainly, God-fearing persons see it as their challenge to increase God's impact on their fellow human beings.

PERSONAL AND PARISH ATTITUDES

In order for those high ideals to be approached, the caring community into which the handicapped will be invited must be prepared. That may include one's entire parish, a small group within that larger one, or only the parish leader. Personal feelings must be clarified and sorted out. When openness displaces defensiveness, annoyance, or abhorrence, the pastor or church can minister.

The task is not a simple one. We classify persons as having sensory, motor, mental, or emotional handicaps. That indicates that they are already seen as something different from the human norm. The words we use to describe them portray their different status in society. It is at the attitudinal level that we prepare to accept those whom we see as different from ourselves. As one handicapped writer has said, "Attitudes toward disabled persons can often be more crippling than the affliction itself" (Colston, 1867, p. 59).

We see this illustrated regularly in the way children interact with each other. They may be very stable and happy and enjoy most of their encounters with one another. But last week's neighborhood clique is disrupted today by excluding one who was part of that group. When that happens, a mini-trauma results. Any child will tell you that the worst possible thing that could happen to her is wanting to play with Sally when Sally wants to play with Joanie. "They don't like me any more; they hate me; they think I'm ugly (or mean, or bossy)," comes the cry. That child's self-image, which may have been soaring in the morning, can plummet in the afternoon on the basis of one such rejection. And yet, the depths of that depression can be instantly cured by a friendly tap at the door and Joanie or Sally inviting her to come out and play!

The way in which past societies have related to disablements has been protrayed quite succinctly (Robinault, 1978, p. 6). In ancient and primitive times handicapped persons were often killed outright. During the Middle Ages they were tolerated as jesters. During the Renaissance asylums were built to isolate them from the rest of society. Modern care began in Switzerland in the eighteenth century, and in the nineteenth century total rehabilitation became the objective.

In society today, handicapped persons want more than rehabilitation. They want to be recognized as unique and valuable. The handicapped movement is becoming a real political force. There are positive results as an awareness of this neglected class of society is raised. But there is also the real possibility that a backlash is starting that could produce negative results (Roberts, 1979). There is the tendency among disadvantaged groups to overemphasize their cause once they begin being heard. It is as if they have been leaning against a door that was stuck for a long, long time. Gentle pushing made no impact, so they leaned harder and harder and finally when the door springs open they temporarily lose their balance. Some feel that the handicapped movement is struggling to maintain its balance now.

However one views the current situation, there is no doubt but that handicapped persons can no longer be seen as human degenerates who need to be destroyed; as walking, living jokes to be tolerated; as obnoxious beings who need to be isolated. Nor are they to be treated as animals who need to be treated and trained. Human progress has made it possible for rehabilitation to take place and for personhood to exist. Residential communities have been formed in several countries that are geared toward incorporating them into society (Lancaster-Gaye, 1972). They and their advocates recognize that their existence will not go away, and the church, in order to be a healing community, must relate to the handicapped as persons, not things.

Persons who anticipate facilitating a group must face these issues in a very personal way. They must practice focusing on the inward person, not the externals. Negative feelings and responses need to be honestly faced and tactfully expressed. (During this learning process, it would be most helpful for the one anticipating group leadership to be supervised by a competent professional.) There is a realization that the best gift the pastor can give to handicapped persons is him/herself. A self-revelation of honesty and openness that includes ups and downs, exuberance and discouragement—that kind of relationship with the pastor, says Colston, can be an example of healthy human contact (1978, p. 59).

As group leaders, pastors will want to empathize with those they are serving. Even if the pastor is not handicapped, similar feelings of rejection, anger, abandonment, exclusion, and loss are faced. The intensity of these feelings will be different for different individuals and their method of expressing them will vary, but it will be most important for the pastor to identify as much as possible with the emotional trauma involved in the lives of the group members.

There is danger here, for the helping person may become too solicitous. As Colston points out, attempting to rescue the handicapped from their own station in life actually communicates a mistrust of their capacity to cope. It reinforces the view of the handicapped person as a victim, helpless and disoriented (ibid., p. 21). This can be offensive to those handicapped persons who want to remain independent, as well as encouraging in the handicapped an undue amount of dependence with a commensurate unwillingness to function to the best of their ability. For example, a disabled husband married for twenty years shocked his wife one day by admitting that he had, over a period of time, appealed to his handicap at moments of irritation or discouragement in order to avoid doing chores around the house! His confession that he used that handicap to obtain sympathy when he felt neglected shocked her, and she recognized for the first time in their marriage that she had not expected of him what he expected of himself. Her continued mothering was most often destructive rather than helpful to him as a person and to their relationship. It allowed him to avoid the real problem that was distressing to him at the moment.

Colston suggests rather what he calls "abiding advocacy", which he goes on to describe as "a continuing, unfailing, persistent standing by, or moving with, or entering into the suffering of handicapped persons" (ibid., pp. xii and xi). That stance allows for honesty without sweetheart stickiness. It does not require a denial of feelings, but challenges the handicapped to face them directly and cope creatively with them. That kind of empathy becomes the key to growth.

This personal evaluation of attitudes, while a necessary part of preparation for group leadership, is also a continuing need. As the group progresses, feelings will recur and subside, and leaders will want to stay aware of this. Then, as the handicapped become integrated into the life of the congregation, periodic circumstances there will cause the issues to resurface, and attitudes as well as facts will need to be discussed. It is as we keep this subject continually before us that our ministry will produce prolonged, positive effects.

HANDICAPPED GROUP ORGANIZATION

One of the first tangible issues to be faced will be a decision as to what kind of group will be formed. Will it be a group of persons with the same handicap or a group of persons with different handicaps? Will it be made up only of families of handicapped persons? Will it be a mixture of handicapped persons and their families? Will any fully functioning persons from the church or community be included? And, once the group has begun, will new members be allowed to join and current members allowed to leave whenever they wish or will there be a set beginning and ending time?

Most of the principles and techniques that will be discussed will apply equally to these various kinds of group structures. However, in an effort to isolate some of the unique distinctions between handicapped persons and others, groups of families and community persons will be discussed in a separate section later in the chapter.

Grouping the Handicapped

There is a tendency of like to cluster together. People with something in common provide support and understanding for each other, so one place to begin would be to form a group of persons with the same handicap. It is possible that several of them would know each other already. Names of potential group members may be made available through support groups, societies, and clinics. They may have had similar backgrounds and they face the same kinds of challenges.

While groups with the same handicap have the advantage of inherent similarities, they lack the perspective added by persons with different handicaps. A mixed group adds the possibility of individuals seeing that those with different handicaps face similar challenges, and, if they are mentally able, it encourages them to empathize with others. They can come to see that others experience similar emotions even though their circumstances differ.

Some of the factors that will be included in deciding which type of handicapped group to have will be: (1) whether the persons involved are able to relate to those with a different set of problems; (2) the type and severity of their handicap; and (3) the availability of persons who want to involve themselves in the group.

Another issue that must be resolved is whether the group will be open or closed. An open group would allow new members to join at any time and current members could decide to stop attending. This sort of group organization may tend to keep up the momentum of the group, for there will always be some new members to nurture, some stable members to provide security, and some older members to contribute experience. It thus allows a "cross-generational" approach with persons at different stages in their growth in the group process.

Frustration may be encountered, however, at the time of introducing new members and saying farewell to those who are leaving. The group has to reorient itself at those times and reidentify its goals and purposes. There may be groups of persons who get along especially well, and when that reidentification takes pace they no longer feel the intense closeness that existed before. These disadvantages need to be weighed against the advantages of having the group always available for incoming persons and not requiring that current members remain indefinitely.

The writer remembers one parting that was particularly poignant. The group had been officially an open-ended one, but the same individuals had been together for several months. The spark plug of that circle of close friends was a young woman. She was very open and expressive of her feelings. At times when she was discouraged, she was not afraid to express depression. At other times, when she was happy and things were going well, she could whip the world! In the same way, she was very supportive of her fellow group members. She not only encouraged them while in session but also spent a lot of time socializing with them away from the group meetings. They found her a welcome refuge in times of discouragement, and a phone call or visit with her was a real boost. The time came when she decided there were others who could fill her role in the group and her own interests were no longer centered there as they once were. Emotionally she was much better able to cope with the ongoing limitations of her disability, and she wanted to turn her attention to other things of importance to her. When she announced her wish to quit coming, stony silence fell over the room. The grief that her leaving engendered had comparatively long-lasting results. In the next several weeks, several other group members began examining their own progress and decided that they, too, were now willing to step out on their own. Within a month, over half of the members of that particular group had changed and others had taken their places. It really is true that no group that meets together today is ever the same again. And that is particularly so of open-ended ones. The group had accomplished one of its major objectives: that of preparing members to face the world realistically and rise to new challenges.

A closed group is one that would begin and end on certain dates. There would be no new members allowed during that period and present members would stay by till the end. This type of organization may avoid some of the trauma of saying farewell and does bypass the reorientation required in introducing new members. The entire group can thus experience the process or life of the group in its entirety.

However, because of the measured amount of time available, more specific goals will need to be established, and the group excludes itself from taking on new members until the prearranged sequence is completed. Also, because everyone in the group knows subconsciously that they will only be together for a specified period of time, personal attachments and deep, emotionally supportive relationships are less likely to form. It is as if the individuals in the group are protecting themselves from the pain of separation and loss, so they refuse to involve themselves very deeply. This can have its advantages in some set tings, but often the handicapped need to experience caring and commitment. In either open or closed groups, it is important that these issues be discussed. As has been mentioned, the handicapped already have suffered great losses and tend to be very sensitive to rejection. Separation from either individual group members or the entire group is another potential trauma for them, and the psychological dynamics involved need to be explored.

GOALS AND PURPOSES

The purpose and goals of the group need to be clearly identified. The type of group that is established suggests some of those goals at its inception. It may be planned for sharing mutual concerns and ideas. It may be for social interaction of those with similar interests. It may be intended to teach them a way in which they can cope with their handicap. It may be a place for them to socially contact others in similar circumstances. It may be an occasion for emotional catharsis and growth.

Whatever the case, those goals need to be clearly identified. They will determine much of what takes place in the group itself and also what methods and techniques are used to bring that about. Colston points out that in the case of handicapped persons who have experienced loss, a supportive therapy supplemented by behavior modification is the indicated approach. He suggests that insight-oriented therapy is not appropriate (ibid., pp. 60-61). Colston here refers to a kind of counseling that tends to be rationally oriented. The value of this approach is that clients are led to *understand* themselves and their behavior. In contrast to this, reality therapy (alluded to in the following paragraph) is more directed toward a cause-to-effect discussion of behavior rather than an attempt to understand the underlying reasons for it. It is certainly true that in the early stages of coping with a handicap one would want to establish a strong base of caring and acceptance, and behavior modification is one approach that might be used.

It is also evident that for those persons without specialized skills, working with the severely handicapped or mentally and emotionally disabled may be more challenging than working with those with motor or sensory handicaps. While working with autistic children, Hubert Coffey and Louise Wiener did not handle deep personal problems in the group; they dealt with those individually. Their groups were primarily reality-oriented (Coffey and Wiener, 1967, pp. 89-90).

From these and other examples we can learn that pastorally-led groups might most beneficially begin by creating acceptance and support. Then they may move beyond that to encouraging motivation toward more successfully coping with the environment. Whether that is done through the techniques of behavior modification, reality therapy, or any of a number of other approaches will need to be determined on the basis of the complexion of the group, its goals and purposes, and the skills and interests of its leader and members.

A distinction needs to be made between counseling and psychotherapy. Unless the pastor has received considerable advanced training, psychotherapy should not be the focus of these groups. When Colston talks about support groups, he is not indicating deep involvement in the group members' pasts nor the unconscious parts of their present lives. An easy rule of thumb might be that the kinds of groups about which we are speaking would concern themselves with present, conscious material. That, coupled with supervision from the group leader, should provide some protection from the group's involving itself too deeply in matters that it is not competent to resolve.

Trotzer made an excellent graph delineating the differences between different kinds of groups. It illustrates well how they actually function on a continuum and also identifies some ways in which different types can be defined.

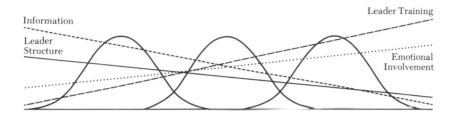

Information

Leader Training

Leader Structure

Emotional Involvement

Group Guidance	Group Counseling	Group Psychotherapy
1. Preventative	1. Remedial	1. Reconstructive or
2. Developmental	2. Normal individuals	reeducative
3. Personally relevant information	3. Thoughts, feelings, and behavior evaluated	2. Personality change
4. Cognitive	4. Problem-oriented	3. Focused support
5. Environmental emphasis	5. Focus determined by members	4. Past history included
6. Presentation and discussion	6. Situational (organized as needed)	5. Conscious and unconscious awareness
7. Leader-directed	7. Relationship important	6. Deep neurotic conflicts, deviant behavior, or severe emotional problems
8. Topic-oriented	8. Empathy and support stressed	7. Individuals considered sick
9. Planned activities	9. Tendency toward homogenity (common problems)	8. Long duration
10. Skills	10. Verbal techniques	9. Homogeneous or heterogeneous
11. Common goals	11. Feelings and needs emphasized	10. High emotional involvement
	12. Conscious awareness	11. Depth analysis and exploration
	13. Leader facilitates	12. Primarily verbal techniques
	14. Present oriented	13. Individual development primary
	15. Nonmedical setting	14. Leader facilitates and directs as needed
	16. Relatively short longevity	

Group Guidance, Group Counseling, and Group Psychotherapy (Trotzer, 1977, p. 20)

Coffey and Wiener talk about areas of emphasis in their autistic children's groups. They identify them as: (1) the relationship of each participant with a therapist; (2) building the ego of each participant; (3) catharsis and reality testing; (4) interpretation and insight; and (5) the social interaction produced by group dynamics (Coffey and Wiener, 1967, pp. 89-90). We might add a sixth area of emphasis: (6) the spiritual growth of each participant. These would apply nicely to any group setting as identifiable objectives.

Another real value of church-sponsored groups is that they demonstrate the caring of the church toward the handicapped. These alienated persons need to be tangibly reminded that the church is concerned for them, that there are individuals within the institution who want to be redemptive and healing in their relationships to the disabled. These kinds of activities can also sensitize the religious community to the values and needs of handicapped persons. If the parish is initially involved in the establishment and support of such groups, the group leader might well take it as a special task to communicate the progress and value of this experience.

THE PASTOR'S LEADERSHIP ROLES

The personality of the group leader will probably have more to do with the degree of success enjoyed by the group than any other human factor. The group leader comes as the ambassador of the caring community and ultimately as the representative of the caring Creator. As that individual is an empathetic, patient, flexible, spontaneous, and honest individual, confidence, enthusiasm, and healing will tend to result (Knowles, 1964, pp. 43-44). In their relationship to group members, skilled leaders will consciously develop trust, acceptance, respect, warmth, communication, and understanding (Trotzer, 1977, pp. 11-12). No matter what skills are used or how thoroughly organized things are, if the leader is not consciously concerned about developing these traits, the impact of the group will be hampered.

It is quickly evident that these characteristics and personality traits tend to be more person-oriented than data oriented. As leaders become more concerned about sharing information than getting in touch with persons, their effectiveness as therapeutic agents decreases. Group counseling leaders need to maintain an active, vibrant concern for others. A ministry of this type is directed to people, and information takes second place to relationships.

Some may wonder if they can be effective leaders of handicapped groups without being handicapped themselves. Absolutely they can! But it is also a challenge. In order to work effectively with the handicapped (or any group of individuals that is different from one's self), the leader needs to focus much early attention on understanding those whom he wishes to help. Personal attitudes of the leader have already been discussed and those are of primary importance. The leader might also spend time, inside the group and out, asking questions and listening to those to whom such ministry is directed. There is no substitute for active, careful listening in coming to understand and feel with another.

That is not to say that information and skills are not important. Trotzer outlines specific ways in which group leaders can act, react, and interact skillfully (ibid., pp. 79-85). Erroneous ideas need to be corrected; accurate information needs to be shared. Certainly the group leader will not want to foster a continuation of misrepresented facts by remaining silent. Still, relationships take precedence.

A pivotal issue here is the type of role leaders see as appropriate to their function. Those who picture themselves as resource persons may lean heavily on the information aspect of the group purpose. There are advantages in this role. It takes away the insecurity of the group by identifying an authority. There is one who knows and is willing to share that knowledge.

There are liabilities associated with this plan as well, and those must be guarded against. The group may come to assume that the leader is the answer machine and may relate to the leader more as a computer than as a person. The leader also needs to define his/her task clearly. Is he/she to lead, to facilitate only, to help the group find the material and resource persons that exist, or to fill the complete leadership role? Leaders must not let the authority associated with this role overwhelm them. They need to continually remind themselves of their strengths and limitations and be open with the group about both. This sort of role may also create strong dependency syndromes with group members. Leaders will find it useful to state their limitations of time and intensity of involvement with the individuals in the group.

Other leaders may be more comfortable being directors. Director-type leaders will help set the parameters of the group task. They will see their function as an organizational, administrative one. They can help the group stick to the subject and integrate new persons who become involved. This approach tends to be more authoritarian and thus may provide an added measure of security for group members who need a stable, parental image.

There are hazards, however, to an authoritarian approach in any relationship, and especially so with the handicapped. They already feel helpless and powerless, and while some may like the security and strength provided by an authoritarian leader, others will only be reminded of their own impotence. This may trigger feelings far beyond their response to the leader, feelings about their handicap and life situation in general. If they are not expressive or are not secure in their relationship with the leader, these feelings may not be communicated, but still they may be present to undermine the personal growth of that individual and the progress of the group as a whole.

Another role that might be played by leaders is that of facilitator. Facilitators encourage group responses. They will be alert to unexpressed messages. They share power with others for subject selection, appropriateness, and direction of the group; they encourage everyone to participate. There are advantages to the facilitator role. It is not so likely to become authoritative or foster dependence. It allows individuals and the group as a whole to develop an identity and encourages individual growth. However, because of the lack of strong leadership, it may tend to create power struggles among group members and could lead to feelings of insecurity and lack of direction.

Group leaders could also be mediators. They may see themselves as the bridge between different members of the group, between handicapped persons and their families, between the fully functioning and the handicapped, or between the church and handicapped persons. In that role, the leader becomes the unifier, the one who awakens the awareness of individuals and groups to each other.

It may not be necessary or possible for these different leadership roles to be acted out in isolation from each other. There are positive and negative aspects to each. The needs and abilities of the group with which one works must be remembered. Leadership roles can be adapted to the personality and potential of each group. Those with more insight and motivation can have that growth potential encouraged. Those who need more explicit direction and encouragement may need a more structured leadership approach. The important thing to remember is that *the group exists for the healing of the members, not for the sake of the leader.* Thus, the leadership role ought to be adapted to encourage the most possible growth for the individual group members.

SUBJECT MATTER

One premise for encouraging the group counseling of handicapped persons is that there is need to encourage their social interaction. Attention will doubtless be centered on that issue as the group begins to function. The relationship of the members in the group to each other will provide both a model for and a reflection of other relationships outside that setting. The way in which members communicate the presence or lack of defensiveness, honesty, spontaneity, sensitivity—all those things that have to do with our relationship to others—would be good material for group discussions. The relevancy of these discussions will increase proportionally as they become personal to the individuals in the group rather than intellectual discussions of theory. The degree to which that takes place will depend on the skill of the leader and the type of group involved.

DISCUSS OR REFER?

Social relationships are an outgrowth of the individual's view of himself or herself. Thus, some attention needs to be paid to the status of the individual. If the group is not a therapeutic one and deep individual problems are surfaced, it would be best to refer those individuals for private counseling. But the group cannot ignore the needs of its members.

The individual life is made up of four basic components: mental, emotional, physical, and spiritual. All are directly related to the others, and a handicap in any one of those areas affects the others. In discussing those areas of concern in the group, leaders need to be alert so as not to go beyond the limits of their own competency.

For example, we might assume that the religious leader has particular expertise about the spiritual component. Because human beings function as a unit, we ought to be acquainted with the interfacing between the spiritual and the physical, emotional, and mental, too. But those other three areas may not be the prime focus of the leader's ability.

That does not suggest that the religious group leader cannot work with groups of individuals who are mentally, emotionally, or physically handicapped, but it does point out that we are not qualified to *treat* mental, emotional, and physical handicaps. We can provide a supportive environment in which the ramifications of those handicaps can be discussed, in which grace and acceptance and forgiveness are experienced. Those responses are appropriate. Going beyond that and exploring the physical ramifications of a physical handicap, the emotional ramifications of an emotional handicap, or the mental implications of a mental handicap requires the referral, consultation, or supervision of a professional in those fields.

CONSULTANTS

Experts in various fields should be invited during a session of the handicapped group to discuss particular questions that have been raised. Let us use the subject of sexuality as an example. Here we face not only the need for information, but also the need for constructive behavior.

Bringing a group of individuals together to share their mutual concerns, joys, and frustrations, encouraging them to share their feelings frankly and honestly to teach them the legitimacy of being spontaneous and caring, invites the possibility of romantic attachments. If they are mentally or emotionally handicapped, the maturity of those attachments may leave something to be desired. The general population may consider these individuals unable to make responsible choices about expressing their sexuality. It has occasionally been the practice to sterilize those who are physically mature but mentally or emotionally disabled. This, it was thought, would prevent unwanted pregnancies and the birth of potentially handicapped offspring, or even the birth of normal children who could not be parentally cared for. Recent legal decisions, however, have brought that practice into serious doubt. Now we must cope with the sexual drive of those who have not been prepared to use it responsibly.

For those who are physically handicapped, on the other hand, there may be the frustration of avoiding closeness with others because of a perceived inability to respond or perform in a traditional sexual way. Even for the fully functioning, sexual impotence is an ominous fear. Sexuality often is the symbol of the individual's ability to be creative, spontaneous, responsive, assertive, and accepting. Accurate, thorough information is necessary.

These issues are vital and a real concern to the handicapped; they must be approached sensibly. It may be that the group leader will not have the knowledge or expertise to do that, and if the issue is raised, it would be a most appropriate time to invite some other authority to visit and deal with those questions. A religiously oriented group is an especially appropriate place for that to be done, as the moral responsibility that a religious background can give is a necessary component for these discussions. The pastoral group leader can complement such a presentation very well.

DISCUSSING LEVELS AND PATTERNS

In the group, there will be a tendency to communicate on different levels. One way in which that might be illustrated is as a pyramid (see illustration, page 87).

The most superficial level on which communication takes place is the level of facts. Facts cannot be argued; they are apparent to everyone. They raise no controversy, and they will not be disputed. Those who talk only on this level never learn much about each other, but avoid people by talking about things.

The second level of communication is the level of ideas or opinions. Here there is the possibility for disagreement, so to share ideas

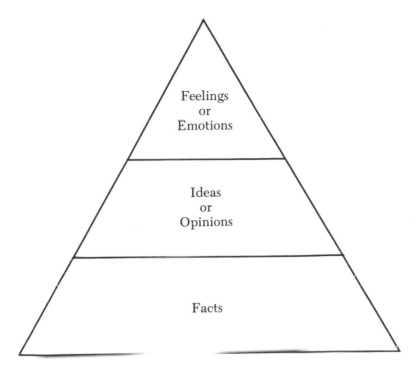

Levels of Communication

and opinions requires some personal risk. The individual becomes vulnerable; controversy could arise. But, because of those very risks, the potential closeness between individuals is increased.

The third level of communication is the level of feelings or emotions. Here there is greater self-revelation. One must not only perceive others' inner responses, but also be willing to share them. That can only take place after trust and acceptance are established. But, again, because of the great risks of rejection and scorn as one reveals deep feelings, there is also the greater possibility of closeness and intimacy.

Because many handicapped have been made fun of, berated, rejected, avoided, and ignored, they have reason to be overly cautious about making themselves vulnerable. The risks of discussing their feelings and emotions may be terrifying, or they may find sharing opinions frightening. Here the acceptance and belonging of the group can provide one of its most valuable services.

The very existence of the group implies that no one's handicap is severe enough to exclude him/her from this social contact. Each was invited, and it's great to be chosen! As members share more and more present and personal information about themselves and see that they are not scorned or rejected for it, a door cracks open. They begin to expose the parts of their lives that are most painful, and festering sores caused by social wounds are opened. When the agony of the feelings is not reinforced but heard with care and empathy by the group, healing begins.

As group members develop confidence in each other, the leader will want to encourage the sharing of more vulnerable conversations. Again, the best way to do that is by modeling. Leaders who are willing to be honest in sharing their own ideas and feelings will engender that behavior.

This is not to suggest that it is inappropriate or unhelpful to have factual discussions, too. The handicapped and their families have many concrete challenges that could well be discussed in the group. Information sharing can be of real benefit to those with similar questions and is certainly legitimate. The illustraton of sexuality, above, is an example. But information sharing in itself will not provide the emotional and social growth that sharing opinions and feelings—especially the latter—will provide.

GROUP LIFE

Every group of people will be comprised of several personality types. There will be those in the group who will tend to be quiet and withdrawn. Others will be very outgoing and gregarious. Some may even attempt to take control of the group, either to satisfy their own needs for leadership, as a defensive maneuver to reduce their tension, or to genuinely spark interest and fellowship. Whatever the case, the leader needs to be alert to the different individuals in the group and, in accord with their wishes, incorporate them in the group system so as to develop a coherent whole.

Fear and Excitement of Newborn. Early in the life of the group, as individuals are just meeting each other and deciding what the function and purpose of the group will be, there is real fear and excitement. It will be important during this time for the leader to help everyone relax, feel comfortable, and gain a sense of security as soon as possible. Being specific about the reason for the group's existence will help. Introductions are vital and might include feelings as well as facts. They provide a means of relieving anxiety and initiating interaction. It might be useful to talk about the anxiety, to recognize it as a group, but not to dwell on that fear. Get right into the program that has brought the group together.

Creativity and Energy of Youth. After the initial anxiety stage, group enthusiasm begins to mount. The leader will want to recognize that, help group members discover the energy created by that enthusiasm, and focus and expand on it. During this period of time, trust in each other and in the group will be growing. Help group members verbalize that trust. Productivity will be increasing. The task for which they have come will begin to be dealt with, and ideas and feelings will be shared.

Reaching Out of Maturity. After a period of time this enthusiasm and energy of youth will become "normal" for the group. The focus is taken for granted. Trust will become old hat. Friendship is becoming more important than the reason for that friendship. Initially the group will have been very productive for personal reasons. The individuals who have come will be greatly benefited. As time goes on, they will expand their views beyond themselves and begin to talk about sharing what they have learned with others. They will become witnesses in that sense and less self-centered—an indication of maturity.

Atrophy of Age. After the period of productivity passes, personal and group enthusiasm begins to wane. Distractions will come. Individuals may begin to miss group meetings as boredom sets in. It will be harder to keep the group on the track; they will tend to wander in their discussions. More frequent recontracting will be necessary. Trust in the group still exists, but there will be less personal involvement on the part of individual members. Help them come to the feeling of a healthy closure. If they quit attending, phone them. This is a critical time for persons with handicaps. They have experienced severe losses already in their lives and to let this one take place without facing it and discussing it thoroughly would be a disservice. Closed groups may have less of a tendency to be traumatized by this stage than open-ended ones. While open-ended groups may not have such a distinguishable sequence as closed groups, the individual group members and the group as a whole needs to be encouraged to discuss what is taking place, to recognize the dynamics of their interaction and deal with that in a healthy, honest way.

GROUP COUNSELING OF FAMILIES

Imagine a normal, healthy, young couple exuberant over the prospects of a soon-to-be-born second child. The pregnancy progressed normally until the last several weeks, when there were times of discomfort and some gnawing anxiety. A specialist was consulted and found that there was cause for concern about a possibly abnormal child. The birth was not a pleasant one, and the child was indeed abnormal. The parents were told that the baby had Down's Syndrome. At that moment of shock, physicians and other hospital personnel were very supportive and encouraged this frightened mother and father by telling them happy stories of other parents who had faced this same dilemma and received much help and support. They were told that there were places where the child could receive needed care and that the child could grow to be a healthy, happy family member.

All that was true, but it did not take away the agony of the coming days and weeks. The parents fluctuated between hope and despair. One moment they tried to convince themselves that their baby boy was really not severely affected, seemed to be developing very nicely, and perhaps would be able to lead a normal life. At others times they were despondent as they recognized his increasing mongolism. Friends and family tried to be comforting but could not know, without experiencing it, the loneliness and isolation this couple faced. In the years that followed, normal siblings became embarrassed by their ugly brother and felt abnormal by association.

During all of those months and years of agony and hardship, this family was a prime candidate for support groups. They poignantly illustrate that it is not only the handicapped but also the social structure surrounding them that is traumatized. Families, too, need group support and encouragement to motivate a creative coping with their life reality. With fear and desperation they face the prospects of a life attached to a dependent offspring. They can hardly anticipate their child's future with joy.

Siblings and relatives experience concerns similar to those of the handicapped. While the problem may not be as physically present in their lives, interrupting sleep, work, and meal schedules, it does disorient family activities, encroach on family vacations, and present a gnawing fear. This couple could well have said what was expressed by another: "Perhaps the greatest help we ever had at this stage was to talk about it to parents of other handicapped children; the parents of normal children either feel sorry or close their minds entirely" (Younghusband, et al, 1970, p. 66).

Establishing a setting in which that kind of sharing takes place can become a real service. Families of the handicapped need a supportive environment in which they can express and explore the restrictions, isolation, frustration, and resentment disability has imposed on them. A sharing of facts and others' methods of handling the challenges of their handicapped relatives can also be most beneficial.

It may be worthwhile to create a mixed group of handicapped persons and families. In that setting, both the handicapped and their families could be benefited by the mutual concerns and reflection of others. It would allow both the handicapped and the fully functioning family members to see how other members of their family relate to a larger social circle.

The same principles of group organization, identification of goals, establishment of leadership roles, and choice of subject matter would be applicable to these sorts of groups as to groups restricted to handicapped persons. And one might also anticipate that groups with this sort of participants would experience the same type of group process as others.

Such groups might become a forum for discussing how the rest of the community could be informed of the needs of handicapped persons and their immediate families. The church or community may become aware of unique ways in which they can share the strain of long hours of taxing care and supervision by relieving parents and family for periods of time for shopping trips, evenings out, and weekends away. Thus a sharing of feelings, which is a benefit in itself, might also effect a change in the causes for some of those emotions.

GROUP RESOURCES

There are many books that deal with group dynamics and counseling. Robert Leslie (*Sharing Groups in the Church*, 1971) gives good examples of Biblically-oriented groups and the group use of Scripture. Lowell Colston (1978, p. 23) points out how valuable that can be in a religious setting where a pastorally-oriented person can use Scripture, prayer, and devotional reading with great effectiveness. Ray Merritt and Donald Whalley's book (*The Group Leader's Handbook*, 1977) is not technical, but has specific outlines for the formation and maintenance of groups. It becomes a good guide for the new group leader who is looking for specific ideas. Alfred Benjamin (*Behavior in Small Groups*, 1978) does an excellent job of explaining the group process and leading the inexperienced through a thoughtful preparation for group leadership. James Trotzer's book (*The Counselor and the Group: Integrating Theory, Training, and Practice*, 1977) is more technical than Merritt and Whalley's. It has excellent theory as well as practical suggestions for why a group functions the way it does and how to make it work better. County and national agencies can be of real service, too.

SUMMARY AND CONCLUSIONS

We have seen how Jesus recognized that to heal a handicapped person most often required more than a private service. Since the disabled are part of society, the social structure in which they exist must be healed as well. There is real value in counseling handicapped persons and their families as groups. Since the attitudes of others are nearly as crippling as the handicaps themselves, a group setting gives all a chance to reflect on others' perceptions of them and others' ways of approaching similar difficulties. These groups provide a way for the church to express its caring concern and also to become sensitized to the value and needs of the handicapped.

The church is in a unique position to provide that kind of healing. Church members are, after all, ambassadors of the Great Healer whose wish is to restore all human beings to healthy relationships with each other and with Him. They can provide the concepts of grace and forgiveness so necessary to the formation of a healthy self-identity and rapport with others.

In order to be effective, however, the church as a community and the helping persons within it must face their attitudes squarely. The handicapped must not be seen as needing extinction, as jestors, as candidates for isolation or even just rehabilitation. The handicapped want to be persons and must be seen as unique and valuable in their own right and not as things who are disabled. When negative attitudes are faced and controlled, empathy, understanding, and honesty can take their place and provide a fitting environment for a supportive, healing group.

Several kinds of groups are possible: persons with the same handicap, persons with different handicaps, families of the handicapped, a mixture of handicapped and their families, open-ended or closed groups. Whatever the composition of the group, its goals and purposes must be clearly identified. The leader must establish a clear concept of the role he or she is going to play.

Subject matter for group interaction can be drawn from the social needs that are so prevalent among the handicapped. Those social needs arise because of individual needs—physical, mental, emotional, or spiritual. While recognizing the limitations of skill and expertise, the group leader will want to encourage a frank discussion and interaction in all of these areas.

The group will probably pass through predictable stages of development. Initial anxieties will be replaced with enthusiasm and productivity and a healthy concern for others before group interest begins to diminish.

Dynamic interaction with groups of handicapped persons and their families can be a rewarding, two-way encounter. It can provide outlets for mutual care and understanding. It can engender self-motivation and improvement. It open the windows between two cloistered groups who need each other.

BIBLIOGRAPHY

Benjamin, Alfred. *Behavior in Small Groups.* Boston: Houghton Mifflin Company, 1978.

Coffey, Hubert S., and Louise L. Wiener. *Group Treatment of Autistic Children.* Englewood Cliffs, N.J.: Prentice-Hall, 1967.

Colston, Lowell G. *Pastoral Care with Handicapped Persons.* Philadelphia: Fortress Press, 1978.

Dexter, Beverly Liebherr, Ed.D. *Special Education and the Classroom Teacher.* Springfield, Ill.: Charles C. Thomas, 1977.

Empey, L. Jane. "Clinical Group Work with Multihandicapped Adolescents." *Social Casework* 58:10 (December 1977):593-599.

Humes, Charles W., Jr. "A Novel Group Approach to School Counseling of Educable Retardates." *Training School Bulletin* 67 (November 1970): 164-171.

Knowles, Joseph W. *Group Counseling.* Philadelphia: Fortress Press, 1964.

Lancaster-Gaye, Derek, ed. *Personal Relationships, the Handicapped, and the Community.* Boston: Routledge & Kegan Paul, 1972.

Larson, Bruce, et al. *Groups That Work: The Missing Ingredient.* Grand Rapids, Mich.: Zondervan Publishing House, 1967.

Leslie, Robert C. *Sharing Groups in the Church.* Nashville, Tenn.: Abingdon Press, 1971.

Merritt, Ray E., and Donald D. Whalley. *The Group Leader's Handbook.* Champaign, Ill.: Research Press Company, 1977.

Roberts, Steven V. "Backlash Trims Gains of Handicap Movement." New York Times News Service, May 15, 1979.

Robinault, Isabel P. *Sex, Society, and the Disabled.* New York: Harper & Row, Publishers, 1978.

Trotzer, James P. *The Counselor and the Group: Integrating Theory, Training, and Practice.* Monterey, Calif.: Brooks/Cole Publishing Company, 1977.

White, Ellen G. *The Desire of Ages.* Mountain View, Calif.: Pacific Press Publishing Association, 1970.

Younghusband, Eileen, et al, eds. *Living With Handicaps.* London: National Children's Bureau, 1970.

Thompson U. Kay

6

Pastoral Care of the Hearing Impaired

Some fourteen million persons in the United States currently have hearing disorders, two million of whom are profoundly deaf. The need to minister to the deaf and hearing impaired is immense. The deaf have specific needs and desire to live a normal, productive life.

It is very important that hearing people be aware of the needs of deaf and hearing-impaired people. Being deaf means more than the inability to hear sounds. Other factors limit the development of deaf children into adulthood as well. It is important for hearing people, interested Christians, to understand these factors and their implications.

The first of these problems deals with deaf individuals' difficulties in mastering language and the effects of the resulting communication limitations on many other aspects of their development. A second, obviously related problem is the insensitivity of hearing individuals toward the impact of early severe hearing loss, and the debilitating ramifications of such lack of empathy.

To be isolated from the human voice is to be isolated from spoken language. The hearing are able to build up an early mastery of the sound, shape, and sense of their language. The profoundly deaf—those with no functional response to speech—usually present an entirely different picture. Unless they have deaf parents, they probably have not acquired a language naturally and automatically. Without intensive compensatory training toward a visual language acquisition, they may be totally nonverbal as well as nonvocal; they may even be unaware that such things as words exist. Typical deaf children, although of normal intelligence, find their range of experience constrained by communication limitations. They suffer, relative to hearing children, from a lack of opportunity to interact fully with and manipulate their environment in meaningful ways. Although deafness itself may have no effect on intellectual potential, the deafness will lead to impoverished communication skills that may limit development severely unless the children are provided compensatory tools.

DEAFNESS

Deafness, in its dictionary definition, is the "state of being unable to hear sounds." Deafness means much more, however, than mere soundless existence to the people affected by it. Factors caused by deafness either directly or indirectly influence the deaf individual's development socially, emotionally, and educationally, and affect his involvement with the world. Several types of deafness are defined here:

Congenital deafness. Congenital deafness is deafness which occurs before or during birth. Congenital deafness is caused either by illness in the mother (e.g., rubella during pregnancy), heredity, or injury sustained at birth.

Adventitious deafness. Adventitious deafness is deafness which occurs in the individual born with normal hearing but who later loses his hearing through sickness or injury. This type is also called "acquired deafness."

Prelingual deafness. Prelingual deafness is deafness which occurs in the child before normal language development has been established.

Postlingual deafness. Postlingual deafness is deafness which occurs in the child after normal verbal language development has been established. In one context the prelingual are called deaf and the postlingual are called deafened.

Conductive hearing loss. Conductive hearing loss results from impairment of the external or middle ear. This impairment may be caused by foreign objects in the ear, perforations of the eardrum, allergies and other respiratory problems which interfere with the functioning of the eustachian tube, or repeated infections in the middle ear which restrict movement of its three small bones. These conditions hinder conduction of sound to the inner ear mechanism. Such deafness should first be directed to an otolaryngologist (ear, nose and throat specialist) for possible medical and/or surgical treatment.

Sensorineural hearing loss. Sensorineural hearing loss is impairment of the nerve cells in the inner ear (cochlea) and in the nerve pathway to the brain, which may be caused by illness, injury, or hereditary factors.

Otosclerosis is a unique bone disease that affects the bony capsule surrounding the inner ear. This bone, normally the hardest in the body, becomes invaded by a different kind of soft bone cell tissue which grows intermittently and then becomes hard again. The most common site for the growth of this new bone is the region around the footplate of the stapes (stirrup), one of the small, sound-conducting bones in the ear.

Other causes of sensorineural hearing losses include bacterial or viral infections. Typhoid fever and diphtheria are two bacterial diseases which probably affect the ear remotely through the toxins formed by the bacteria in either the gastrointestinal tract or the respiratory tract. The result is more or less complete degeneration of the organ of Corti (the location of the nerve cells in the snail-shaped inner ear).

Viral infections, such as mumps or measles, differ from bacterial infections in that the virus is microscopic in size, much smaller than bacteria. The virus can reach the ear from the bloodstream and do its damage directly rather than secondarily through toxin production.

Meningitis is the infection or inflammation of the coverings of the spinal cord ("meninges"). If the infection reaches the inner ear, it may destroy the auditory nerve, the organ of Corti, or most or all of the other delicate auditory structures. Bacterial infection in the inner ear, similar to the infection previously discussed, can lead to total loss of hearing. This infection can begin any time in the first year or two of life.

A blow to the head, or "boxing the ears" of children as a form of punishment can cause severe pain in the middle ear and possible injury to the eardrum and fracture or dislocation of the ossicles (the three small bones in the ear). Blows can also cause permanent damage in the inner ear.

Hereditary factors can cause hearing loss. Genes are the building blocks of heredity and are carried in the chromosomes. The processes by which genes and chromosomes interact to determine the characteristics of the newborn infant are very complex. If these processes are disrupted, congenital deafness may result.

One major cause of congenital deafness is rubella (or "German measles") contracted by the mother during pregnancy, the most dangerous time being between the first and third months. The disease is, for the mother, a mild infection. It has been reported that many mothers who give birth to babies with the virus showed no symptoms of the virus themselves. However, the virus has caused thousands of babies to be born with sensorineural hearing losses, as well as many with multiple handicaps.

Sometimes sensorineural deafness cannot be sufficiently aided by amplification because of the complexity of the loss. However, even in such cases hearing aids are customarily recommended to keep persons in contact with sound.

THE CASE OF MR. PETE

"You had a communication problem yourself, didn't you, Mr. Pete, when you were a boy?"

"What do you mean?"

"Back in St. Catharines, Ontario."

"Oh!" Mr. Pete's mind rolled back to when he was an eight-year-old boy in Canada, recently from Czechoslovakia. His aunt and uncle had brought him to live with them in St. Catharines, and he could not speak or understand a word of English.

It was torture to stand on the sidelines that winter and watch the kids play a road hockey game using sticks, two bricks for a goal, and lots of energy. Pete desperately wanted to play too, but no one could understand him. Pete felt shut out and thought the kids were talking about him. Frustration filled him until he burst into rage, but no one seemed to care.

Then an older boy motioned for Pete. He handed Pete a hockey stick, and Pete threw himself into the action, swinging wildly. Pete whacked one boy across the back, and this resulted in a fist fight.

Pete stood on the same sidelines the rest of the game, glowering. Afterwards the older boy showed Pete how to hold the stick; then he demonstrated some shots. Patient with Pete's first attempts, he gently shook his head at Pete's mistakes and patted Pete on the back for his good moves. Pete felt the warmth of his concern. This made Pete feel worthwhile and gave him confidence. In a few weeks Pete not only learned the rudiments of hockey, but he was picking up some English, too.

By the time Pete was eighteen, he was on a team which was well on its way to a Canadian championship. Several years later Pete became a player for the Chicago Blackhawks hockey team and he has played about thirty years in hockey competition.

Pete was faced with another challenge when he was asked to teach deaf boys hockey. He saw himself standing at the sidelines in St. Catharines years ago. He smiled at a deaf boy, Bob, then gently led Bob onto the ice. Giving the boy his hockey stick, Pete showed him how to hold it, hands a foot and a half apart. With Pete behind Bob, and with his hands on Bob's, both skated together toward a puck on the ice until the deaf boy learned the game.

The experience Pete had with his inability to speak English is similar to the experience the deaf encounter—the isolation, the inability to communicate, and the frustration of trying to express their needs.

THE COUNSELOR'S ROLE

Whether we are asleep, at play, or whatever we are doing, our hearing provides a continual link with the world around us. Our brain continuously (unconsciously) monitors our environment for danger signs and warns us if something amiss is detected. The deaf person does not have this built-in security system. He must rely on his eyes, which function directionally, to do the work of his ears, which function omni-directionally. The deaf are in a world of silence and this cannot be remedied by the use of the eyes.

The problems occurring for deaf persons stem from the inability to communicate with the hearing world. Communication or the lack of it determines, in a major way, the problems the deaf individual must face in his own life and in relating to other people.

Many of the problems deaf adults have today were caused by the traumatic experiences and frustrations of childhood training. These experiences caused feelings of inadequacy, failure, personal inferiority, and even hatred of their own deafness.

As counselors for the deaf in the community, school, or church, we must accept the deaf as people. Our response should always be one of acceptance, loving people the way they are and accepting their unique qualities. We are then in an excellent position to lead them toward Christian maturity.

Considerations in Counseling the Deaf

The counselor should communicate with deaf people on their level. He should not place the deaf person in the awkward, frustrating position of trying to communicate on his level (if this is difficult for the deaf person to do). Many hearing impaired have not had a wide variety of life experiences such as travel or cultural and normal-level educational exposure and therefore do not have a high-level language speech reservoir. The deaf person with a high experience level will have no difficulty communicating with the counselor; but when counselors work with people on a lower experience level they must use language meaningful and clear to the deaf person.

Talk *with* deaf people, not *to* them. Share, interact, give and take. Enjoy what the deaf people have to say, and learn from them. They have much to offer you as you strive to improve your general understanding of deaf people; and, as you work, your language skills will improve.

Make the counseling environment as comfortable as possible for the deaf. Remove anything that produces unnecessary anxiety. For example, it may be well to limit the number of hearing people in the setting.

Learn to listen to deaf people. Hear what they are really saying, not what you think they are saying. If you do not understand something, ask them to repeat it. Do not let false pride prevent your doing so. Their speech is not always intelligible. It can easily be misunderstood. The deaf do not mind repeating and are patient with the hearing person who is really trying to communicate with them.

Love deaf people. Acceptance and love go hand in hand. The love should be *agape* love, loving without necessarily being loved in return. Love overcomes many faults.

Understand the deaf. Try as we might, hearing people have extreme difficulty seeing things as deaf people do. Many deaf people feel we cannot understand them, and in many ways this is true. However, we should work toward developing a good understanding of both their thoughts and feelings on matters affecting them.

One day a deaf lady was visiting in Pastor Griffith's home, sharing with him and his wife her feelings of distrust and frustration with hearing people. The deaf lady said, "Hearing people are so insensitive and cruel, Pastor Griffith; you know how hearing people are!" Then she paused, her eyes widened, her face turned slightly red, and after another pause, she said, "Oh, but you are different, Pastor!" Why? Because Pastor Griffith and his wife had learned to comprehend the frustration and suspicions of the deaf lady and to share her feelings of hurt. They understood, and the deaf lady sensed that understanding.

Help and encourage the deaf toward independence. Counselors for the deaf should always work toward freeing the deaf to become all they can become as they mature. Counselors should encourage the deaf to do things for themselves and to maintain their pride as persons capable of doing so. Too often people unconsciously keep the deaf from developing by doing everything for them unnecessarily.

Lead them. Be a good model of the Christian life. Show the deaf how to find God's will for their own lives. Outline steps for them to follow in order to enrich their lives as Christians. Practice what you preach.

Develop the sense of trust. The deaf person needs to feel that the counselor can be trusted and is dependable. This trust can be developed by keeping secrets the deaf person tells, keeping promises made to him, and giving the best possible answers to his questions.

Encourage self-respect. Workers should help the deaf with constructive supervision rather than ordering them around as children. Harsh criticism can damage the deaf's self-respect. Each person is unique and made in the image of God. It is better to help the deaf person understand God's goodness in an atmosphere of love than to criticize him continuously because he is not measuring up to our standards.

There are times when group counseling can be implemented and this can play a significant part in working with deaf people. In a group counseling situation each person is led to discuss his problems and/or feelings with other members of the group. Some will not do so at first, but, as confidence in the group grows, more will share their feelings.

Deaf people want to be an integral part of society; they want to be heard (especially about subjects they consider important), to have their opinions properly evaluated, to ask questions, to be given reasons, and to have secrets. As a counselor for the deaf, it is your responsibility to give them a chance to do these things.

CHRISTIAN FELLOWSHIP

One of the most common places for individuals to fellowship in a Christian atmosphere is the church. The church is a hospital where sick come to be healed, a school where they learn about life, a place where they may calmly consider their relationship with the Creator. The church is the family of the Saviour, where we gather to share our joys and sorrows and to worship the One who makes that family possible. When the family gathers, it is a time of celebration and interaction, of reaching outward to those who do not yet know the Saviour, and reaching inward collectively to know each other better. It is an atmosphere electrified with love and expectant hope. It provides the perfect environment for growth in all areas of life.

Into this environment we bring the deaf and hearing impaired. We communicate, smile, guide, direct, encourage, praise, accept, and teach them concerning our Saviour, who makes our church family possible. We involve the deaf in meaningful activities—activities that not only teach the deaf about the Saviour, Jesus Christ, but also about themselves as persons. In this way we work toward providing meaningful experiences for the deaf person, experiences which he can relate to and through which he can relate to his Creator and Saviour. We relate to the deaf and this allows the deaf to relate to others. The church family can provide the "missing link" to the needs of the deaf because Christians care.

MODES OF COMMUNICATION

Deafness is an invisible handicap that is not obvious until the individual uses a mode of communication not used by the hearing world at large.

The counselor must be aware that there are various methods of communication with the deaf. It should be noted that there are controversies over the methods, particularly in educational settings. Both the oral approach, which relies on lipreading without any benefit of manual communication, and the total communication approach rely heavily on the use of residual hearing.

Fingerspelling. This uses the twenty-six different single-hand positions representing the twenty-six letters of the alphabet.

Sign Language. A language that uses manual symbols to represent ideas and concepts. The term is usually used to describe the language used by deaf people in which both manual signs and fingerspelling are employed. There are at least five major sign systems including Signed English, Signed Essential English, and Ameslan (American Sign Language). There are also regional variations as markedly different as the regional dialects in the hearing world.

Lipreading, Speechreading. A technique by which one person understands the speech of another without hearing sound, by observing the other person's lip movements and facial expressions. This method is used without employing fingerspelling or the language of signs.

Manual Communication. Communication by use of signs and fingerspelling.

Total Communication. Includes the following: speech, amplification (hearing aids), lipreading, gesturing, signs, fingerspelling, pantomime, reading, writing, pictures, and any other possible means of conveying ideas, language, and vocabulary.

COMMUNICATION PRINCIPLES

Do

1. Learn the manual alphabet and signs. Anyone can learn simple basic fingerspelling in less than half an hour.

2. Learn the deaf person's name or sign. The deaf person's sign is analogous to a CB-er's "handle."

3. Get the deaf person's attention before communicating with him; he/she may need to be tapped lightly on the shoulder.

4. Introduce yourself and use the sign for your name.

5. Keep your face and hands toward the deaf person with whom you are speaking.

6. Maintain eye contact with the deaf person while you are conversing.

7. Speak slowly and clearly with a regular tone of voice. Avoid exaggeration of lip movement. It distorts the speech.

8. Make every attempt to include any deaf person present in any conversation you are having with another hearing individual.

9. Try to make the deaf person at ease in your presence.

10. Refer to the deaf as a deaf person, nonhearing, or hearing impaired.

11. Practice signing at home as a follow-up to learning of correct signs. Practice makes perfect if it is guided correctly.

12. Feel good that you are accomplishing something in your attempt to communicate with the deaf. They feel good when you try.

Do Not

1. Do not refer to the deaf as dumb, deaf-mute, or "deafies."

2. Do not stamp your feet or make inappropriate gestures to get the deaf person's attention.

3. Do not cover up your face or lips with your hands, or turn away from the deaf person's presence when talking to another individual.

4. Do not allow your attention to be diverted by another hearing person.

5. Do not refer to deaf persons as indifferent.

6. Do not treat the deaf adult like a child.

7. Do not stare at the deaf person excessively.

8. Do not ridicule the deaf.

9. Do not be persistent in helping the deaf when help is not needed or wanted.

10. Do not restrict your conversation to business matters; deaf people have feelings, opinions, and a sense of humor like other individuals.

11. Do not become discouraged when you find you have trouble at first in reading what the deaf person is saying (orally or manually).

12. Do not get upset when you find there are regional variations in using sign language which may confuse you in your attempt to communicate with the deaf.

HELPFUL HINTS

1. Deafness is not contagious, and it does not transmit from one person to another; however, it can be hereditary.

2. Deaf people do have a sense of humor.

3. Being deaf does not mean the individual is mentally retarded and cannot be educated.

4. The phrases "deaf-mute" or "deaf and dumb" are very outdated expressions which are offensive to hearing-impaired people. The deaf may not hear, but they can laugh, cry, or produce other sounds. They have intelligence.

5. A deaf person is capable of taking care of himself. He is not physically disabled; he just cannot hear. If he needs help, he will let you know.

6. Some deaf are treated as inferior. If given an opportunity, they can live normal and productive lives.

7. When you meet a deaf person, it does not help to talk loudly to communicate. If you speak in a normal, unexaggerated manner, some deaf persons will be able to understand by lipreading.

8. One of the best ways to work with the deaf and to clear suspicion is with love. The gospel of Jesus Christ should be very eminent in our lives. It is our responsibility to explain the gospel, live it, love it, and share it with our deaf population.

BIBLIOGRAPHY

Ewing, Alexander. *Teaching Deaf Children to Talk.* Washington, D.C.: Manchester University Press, 1964.

Hallowell, Davis, and S. Richard Silverman. *Hearing and Deafness.* New York: Holt, Rinehart, and Winston, Inc., 1970.

Kay, Thompson U. *A Handbook About Deafness.* Lincoln, Neb.: Christian Record Braille Foundation, 1980.

Lloyd, Lyle L. *Communication Assessment and Intervention Strategies.* Baltimore: University Park Press, 1976.

Mikita, Stan. "A Sign from Christ." *Guidepost,* March 1981, pp. 72-82.

Moores, Donald F. *Educating the Deaf: Psychology, Principles and Practices.* Hopewell, N. J.: Houghton Mifflin Company, 1978.

Riekehof, Lottie L. *The Joy of Signing.* Springfield, Mo.: Gospel Publishing House, 1978.

Yount, William R. *An Introduction to Ministry With the Deaf.* Nashville, Tenn.: Broadman Press, 1976.

Roy E. Hartbauer

7

Management of the Misinformed and Uninformed

The pastor is in a unique position when he is convinced that a parishioner is misinformed or uninformed. He is forced into believing and saying that he has information that is more truthful, more rational and reasonable, and more appropriate than the counselee has received from other sources. He needs to approach the situation with questions which include, "Is there actually, based on all available information, a misdiagnosis of the patient by medical and other professionals?" "Is there sufficient evidence to believe that the counselee was not told the truth?" "Were there factors which prevented the counselee's accepting the truth?" "Through what channels was information given?" And most important of all, the pastor must ask if he may be the one who has been misinformed or uninformed.

Let us address the last point first. Several years ago the writer had dinner guests including a pastor and his family and a young married

Readers of this chapter are directed to *The Minister as Diagnostician* by Paul W. Pruyser for an excellent discussion of the pastor in a partnership role with other professionals.

couple. During an after-dinner walk through some houses under construction the pastor was speaking of some of the points a builder had told him to consider in the placement of heating system outlets. As the conversation continued, it was evident to the writer that the placements as the pastor was detailing them were for a significantly different type of architecture and climatic setting. The information that he was giving was both right and wrong—basically wrong because if it had been installed by the young couple where they were contemplating building, the heating system would have been less than satisfactory.

The same principle could be true regarding the handicapped. The pastor may not know, without comprehensive research, that certain information is inappropriate, out of context, or potentially dangerous. He may have received his views from a biased, one-sided perspective. He may have been "brainwashed" by closed-minded, fanatical advocates of a certain school of thought. For example, there are those individuals who are so intense in advocating the oral approach to education of the deaf that they cannot even discuss alternatives to it. These persons will not accept the fact that any method but theirs can be viable. Should the pastor not have been told about the education of the deaf by these individuals, he may have had a broader knowledge of the alternative methods of total communication. Neither the oral nor the "total" approach is the answer in all cases, but rather each case must be considered from many angles. Only when all avenues are known and appropriate criteria applied will the pastor avoid making the type of mistake in his counseling of the handicapped that was made by the pastor discussing the building of houses.

The reader can quickly see that there will be times when the pastor is put in opposition to members of the medical profession and other professionals. He will, in effect, be challenging them. He will at that moment be open to the accusation by assorted persons of attempting to practice another profession without a license. Rightfully, he can be asked, "By what authority do you disagree?" "What gives you the right to contradict?" The pastor needs to have a defense ready. He must be able to give the rationale for his statements. Let us look at this aspect.

Wise and intelligent professionals are willing to admit that they have made mistakes and that it is within the realm of possibility that mistakes will be made again. They know that they are not infallible. They know that some of their colleagues make quick decisions without all the available information or on an initial impression that would have been changed if additional diagnostic workups by appropriate professionals had been done. These professionals also realize that there are factors pastors know that the clients have either intentionally or unintentionally not made known to the others involved in their care. Note that privileged information must remain just that unless there is patient permission to release it. This can be one of the pastor's greatest defenses.

OTHER PROFESSIONALS

It is an unpleasant moment when pastors face the individual who has been uninformed and misinformed by other clergy, either of the same denominational affiliation or of a church with a substantially different theology. We may think at first of the differences of doctrine regarding the state of the dead, permitted (or at least accepted) health practices, codes of conduct, or the actual differences regarding belief in a Supreme Being. The pastor is called on by non-Christians. He must be acquainted with those persons' orientations to life and the Being whom they worship. Yet more than those denominational differences, the pastor comes face to face with misinformation and lack of information that other pastors have given the patient. It can be about anything from the agencies and services in the area to downright falsehoods about either you or your church.

Whether it is another pastor, a physician, or any other professional that you feel has given misinformation or has withheld information from your counselee, you are, in effect, judging him, and this should be done with extreme caution. In this judging you are questioning the integrity, intelligence, training, experience, techniques, and procedures of another person. You are concerning yourself with his logic, his school of thought, and his interpretation of data and materials at hand. You must show concern for every aspect of that individual as well as concern for the handicapped.

When a handicapped person, or his associate, tells us about a fellow professional, be it regarding the individual or his services, we have several major obligations forced upon us, such as to:

(1) Question whether the counselee is being truthful, i.e., (a) Is he purposely not telling the truth? (b) Is he telling you what he believes you expect and want to hear, even if he must make it up or distort truth? (c) Is he conning you in an attempt to get you to do something the other person would not do? (d) Has he misunderstood when there has been no attempt at untruth?

(2) Realize there is a chance that incorrect information is due

solely to insufficient clarification and explanation.

(3) Determine if the person is presenting the "whole truth and nothing but the truth" as viewed through his interpretation, perceptual and intellectual level, prejudice, and personal integrity. His view is prismed by his knowledge of this particular problem and his command of relevant vocabulary. We may also be guilty of assuming that the handicapped person has more knowledge, particularly of vocabulary and terminology, than he actually has.

(4) Ask if it is possible that the information and its interpretations came from the professional to the patient or from the patient to you through a third party who may, in spite of abject ignorance, be anxious to share from his "vast storehouse of knowledge."

Keep in mind that at the time of establishing the presence or absence of incorrect or inadequate information you are comparing and contrasting your own education, experience, integrity, and information with that of other professionals. You are asking for agreements and disagreements. You are comparing similarities and differences and you will be judged on your own qualifications and judgments when you ask for a consultation.

Anyone can make an honest mistake. Show the other person compassion. His error or apparent error is actually a pleasure to help resolve if done in Christian love. In contrast to those who make honest mistakes are the persons (both professional and lay) who give information for diagnosis that is arrived at without viewing the entire problem. It is the same as the story of the blind men and the elephant. Each man equated the part with the whole. Recently a case history reported that the parents of a child had taken him to seven practitioners and centers before they found the true problem. These parents were not "shoppers" who were looking for "smooth sayings" or "miracle" cures. They were perceptive enough to know that all the pieces of the puzzle had not been seen. The confirmed diagnosis was a profound sensorineural hearing loss. The boy had been mislabeled as autistic, mischievous, brain damaged, obstreperous, and mentally retarded by professionals who had made their diagnoses after brief observations of behavior. But they had not sought the reasons for the behavior, namely, that the child could not hear the stimuli presented orally during the administering of standardized tests that required hearing to understand the test procedures. It is fortunate for the pastor that it is almost always another professional from the same diagnostic therapeutic field who has the responsibility of declaring that other professionals are in error.

Who is included among those who give spurious or insufficient information? It may be (1) a fellow clergyman, (2) health team members not trained in the specialty or who are out of date, (3) untrained and unethical merchandisers of supplies and equipment for the handicapped, (4) untrained teachers, (5) zealous and overzealous friends, and (6) grandparents and relatives with good intentions but who do not have all the pertinent facts.

Pastors are to get as much information first-hand or in writing as is possible. Furthermore, pastors should put things in writing. These are personal and legal safeguards.

THE THIRD PARTY

That brings us to the problem of the third party. The pastor really gets much of his information from a third party and often that third party is the patient. The patient relays what the health professional has said, or what the patient thinks was said. In addition, the patient will say what he thinks the pastor wants to hear, or what he wants the pastor to hear. It is up to the pastor-counselor to sort this out.

But more important than the third-party patient is when the third person involved is a parent, son or daughter, or anyone else who gives you information. Any time information goes through another individual it gains another perspective, another sincere concern (in most cases), or another interpretation of the original words. The third person can be honest, self-seeking, vicious, devious, or even a fanatic moralizer. He can be ignorant or incapable of understanding what is involved.

What is the pastor to do? He can (1) determine the intellectual and emotional capacities and stabilities of the third party, (2) question the third party's ego-involvement, or (3) ascertain specific interests of the third party, be they anything from a pure desire to help to conniving to hasten an expected inheritance. Protect yourself by involving the third person in the gathering of information as little as possible, unless it is mandated by law or parent-child relationship.

After all information has been obtained and it is truth as determined by all criteria, we can face another problem. Some people just will not accept facts. Some people will realize truth as such but cannot accept it. Nearly all of us have seen the "shoppers." They are looking for something that their constitutional makeup will let them accept or something that will agree with their preconceptions. We would err, however, if we did not show compassion to the "shoppers" who have been deceived or wronged. They do not know whom to believe. They have followed many leads that have taken them nowhere. This latter group may need psychiatric or psychological attention. They need the tender touch.

There are several types in this group that make pastoral counseling interesting, challenging, and sometimes frustrating. The non-acceptive person has been given an accurate picture of his condition, adequate information, verification by consultants, and competent counseling, yet will not accept the truth. He may be the "know-it-all" who is positive that the diagnosis is not complete. He is the one whose vast knowledge indicates that (1) he *knows* someone is not doing a thorough job, (2) there are factors which have not been brought into focus, or (3) in time the correct diagnosis will be given.

The loudmouth is the first type of "know-it-all." We can be comforted that there are few of these who are handicapped but we do find too many of them in the third-party group. This individual knows more than anyone else and you cannot change his mind. He belittles anyone who does not agree with him, particularly the pastor, no matter how faulty or absent his logic may be. The "know-it-all" is found in all socioeconomic strata. If he is in the lower level he uses his approach to try to climb higher. If he is in the higher level his attitude keeps him there because his word is law.

Quite in contrast to the loudmouth is the quiet, almost self-deprecating type. This is the person who is convinced that there is more than what has been considered.

The third type of "know-it-all" is the one who knows the facts and the truth but also knows he can "get by" doing nothing to help reduce the effects of his handicap. For example, a person may know a hearing aid would help but also knows that he can get by in his own way without one—regardless of the inconvenience to others.

There are some who will not or cannot accept what they are told. This non-acceptance is a type of misinformation or lack of information. The truth is not processed. Truth is distorted or confused. Non-acceptance is a stone wall that blocks out alternatives and closes off all perspectives; it arrests progress.

Now, before we categorically and totally condemn the denying person, we should take a closer look. The truth may have been given too much at a time, with poor tact, or at an inappropriate time. It may be too threatening because the handicapped person does not have his reserves ready to call upon. The timing can be wrong because of his preoccupation with other critical concerns. The truth can be too remote from reality or the person's orientation. Or, it could have been presented to him in a sequence or in a vocabulary the person is ill-prepared to handle. Doubtlessly the reader has had experiences that have been momentarily similar.

On the other hand, the counselee can handle denial by (1) vociferously declaring he never heard things which had been explained in detail, (2) stating that what he has been told does not or cannot exist, or (3) asking the unpleasant to disappear. Denial is not an unqualified sign that a person should be put into psychological counseling. We all go through the initial denial phase when we face an unwelcome, unpleasant experience. Even in instances when we have expected the worst, denial flashes through us momentarily.

You, as pastors, have seen many people deny that they are in need of a Saviour, deny that God (Christ) is real, or deny that their current religious beliefs should be changed to those you have personally found to give a richer and more exciting life.

How long does denial last? When does it become a hindering factor in (re)habilitation? What can be done about it? How do we eliminate this type of "misinformation"?

In the normal person, denial is timed by the patient's inner strength and mechanism for confronting and resolving the unpleasant. Earlier in this chapter we noted that there may be other problems which have a higher priority at the time and they must be resolved first. Denial lasts until the person gets the perspective of his life into focus. He sees how the truth is an integral part of a better way of life. Only after that does denial no longer have the same dynamics as misinformation or noninformation.

Another factor controlling the duration of denial is the counselee's previous experiences in similar situations. The pastor-counselor helps the counselee recall them. He helps the counselee see their relevance to the present situation. He helps the counselee see how acceptance of truth has been beneficial. Let the individual see that to progress he must move beyond denial to resolution stages.

We move now to consider the "misinformation," if we may call it that, of the handicapped person who has been given doctrinal training that differs from yours. The counselee may have been reared with a particular theological training, may be recently converted, may be in the process of receiving Bible studies, or may be searching for a teaching in which he can find a relationship to a Supreme Being that he can claim. In any event, there is a difference between his current beliefs and yours. You, as a minister-advocate of your tenets of faith, feel that the other doctrines are not true. You feel the other teachings are "misinformation" and your proselytic bent commands you to tell what is the *truth*.

Are you calling the advocates of other doctrines liars? Are you questioning their integrity, honesty, ethics, mentality, or emotional stability? Hardly! We cannot condemn a man for believing. We dare not ridicule him for his convictions. We absolutely cannot speak against the clergy of another faith. We can, however, question *what* he believes. The handicapped are just as alert as anyone to our knocking people rather than their convictions. They are attuned to ridicule.

What does religious difference have to do with misinformation? Basically, each minister feels that any interpretation of doctrine that is not the same as his is wrong. Therefore, it is misinformation. Each minister who does not accept the sources of the tenets of another church's faith feels that only his is correct. For example, the Roman Catholic Church bases its teaching on the Holy Scriptures, tradition, and the speaking of the papal chair. Non-Catholics do not accept all of these teachings. Other Christian churches claim prophets or prophetesses that are accepted and believed only by their own adherents. Jewish believers do not accept Jesus Christ as the Messiah; therefore Christians feel they are wrong. Don't forget, there are handicapped persons in all church bodies and religions.

Religious counseling is a primary factor in counseling when there is a handicap. The person's religious faith is the cornerstone for how he faces trauma, resolves guilt, and perceives the future, both until and after death. His relationship to a Supreme Being is the basis for belief in divine strength, healing, and acceptance of situations that cannot be changed. His desire for an intimate, personal oneness with God is the reason that you, a pastor, are there. You are there to bring religious beliefs and reality together. You are there to straighten out his thinking about God. He has, or develops, a belief in you that you will not give misinformation.

He may not believe in you at first. All too often he has observed people who claim a close walk with God who he knows are living hypocritical lives and he wonders about the power of the gospel. He views other people's inconsistent lives as lies and does not want to be like them. We could wish that some ministers' lives had been better examples of what to be rather than what *not* to be. Too many insincere ministers have proclaimed an intense devotion to God and the church. The handicapped want no part of such a charade.

BIBLIOGRAPHY

Barsch, R. *Counseling with Parents of Emotionally Disturbed Children.* Springfield, Ill.: Charles C. Thomas, 1970.

Benjamin, A. *The Helping Interview.* Boston: Houghton-Mifflin, 1974.

Bird, Brian. *Talking with Patients.* Philadelphia: Lippincott Co., 1973.

Buscaglia, L. *The Disabled and Their Parents: A Counseling Challenge.* Thorofare, N.J.: Charles B. Slack, 1975.

Cull, John G., and Hardy, Richard. *Counseling Strategies with Special Populations.* Springfield, Ill.: Charles C. Thomas, 1975.

Hartbauer, R. E. *Counseling in Communicative Disorders.* Springfield, Ill.: Charles C. Thomas, 1978.

Kahn, R., and Caunell, C. *The Dynamics of Interviewing.* New York: John Wiley and Sons, Inc., 1959.

McDonald, E. *Understanding Those Feelings.* Pittsburgh: Stanwix House, 1962.

Messer, Alfred A. *The Individual in His Family: An Adaptational Study.* Springfield, Ill.: Charles C. Thomas, 1970.

Oden, Thomas C., et al. *After Therapy What?* Springfield, Ill.: Charles C. Thomas, 1974.

Pruyser, Paul W. *The Minister as Diagnostician.* Philadelphia: The Westminster Press, 1076.

Richardson, S., Dohrenwend, B., and Klein, D. *Interviewing: Its Forms and Functions.* New York. Basic Books, Inc., 1965.

Satir, Virginia. *Peoplemaking.* Palo Alto, Calif.: Science and Behavior Books, Inc., 1972.

Taylor, F. "Project Cope." In *Professional Approaches with Parents of Handicapped Children,* E. Webster, editor. Springfield, Ill.: Charles C. Thomas, 1976.

Wise, Carroll A. *The Meaning of Pastoral Care.* New York: Harper and Row, Publishers, 1968.

Donald A. Riesen

8

Ministering to the Amputee and the Paralytic

It is the objective of this chapter to help us learn to relate to losses. Losses are painful. In our less-than-perfect world they are also unavoidable. As I see it, life is a continual experience of gains and losses. The gains in life, even though they may be challenging and stressful, are for the most part enjoyable and rewarding experiences. But the losses in life are indeed threatening and can be disastrous and devastating. To a great extent the way in which we choose to relate to both the gains and losses in life determines our outcome, here and for eternity. It is imperative that we endeavor to help those who are feeling the pain and experiencing the grief of loss.

There are many categories of loss. The major categories might be: the loss of persons or personal relationships, the loss of body parts or functions, the loss of material things and positions, and the loss of ideas or the need to change one's way of thinking. Nearly every day we experience losses in one or more of these categories. Fortunately most of these losses are relatively minor and are handled adequately. Our degree of possessiveness plays an important role in the way we relate to the losses of life. Possessiveness is the inability or refusal to accept the prospect of being or doing without persons, body parts and functions, things, and ideas. The greater the tendency to be possessive, the more

114

intense will be our feelings of insecurity and grief when losses occur. On the other hand, those who have developed an unselfish and grateful lifestyle will be better able to cope with losses and changes in their lives.

In the area of gains and losses, Jesus said, "Who will lose his life [will not be possessive of his life and will choose to share it, even to give it up to benefit others] will save it. But whosoever will save his life [be possessive of his life, desiring to keep only for himself all his gains] will lose it." One of our greatest challenges as teachers and pastors is to help those we serve to truly enjoy the assets and gains of life, but to face our humanism realistically, and thus see things, persons, and relationships as only temporary blessings to be shared, not to be selfishly hoarded.

COMMON PSYCHOLOGICAL RESPONSES TO CRITICAL LOSSES

With this introduction, we turn to a few of the terms commonly used and the psychological responses commonly seen in those who have sustained critical losses of limb or function. It is important as we choose to play a supportive role in the lives of those who are experiencing or have experienced the loss of body parts (as in the case of amputation or paralysis) that we become acquainted with these responses and terms.

1. *Crisis.* Crisis refers to an unsettling or threatening event that creates emotional disequilibrium. It calls for adaptive responses that require the amputee or paraplegic to examine new ways of relating to life and dealing with change. Pastoral support at such a time of crisis is aimed at helping the individual cope with the immediate and overwhelming sense of loss. This is pain at its worst. It begins to be felt in the life of the patient almost simultaneously with physical pain, and continues to bring discomfort long after the physical pain is arrested. This is the pain we humans experience when we are stopped in our tracks, when we are no longer in control, when we need to ask for help, when we suddenly realize we will never again be exactly as we were. This crisis presents a whole new world with lots of questions involving our identity, our families, our God, our future, etc. The ministry of "standing by," of shepherding (standing alongside), is so vital during this crisis period. Answers are not as important as presence. We need not feel we must have all the answers to the myriads of difficult questions that crowd the minds of hurting persons. They must feel love and support, acceptance and understanding. In most cases answers and explanations cannot reverse the loss and may even complicate feelings

concerning it. During this critical crisis stage of loss the process of grief
will begin.

2. *Grief.* Grief is a definitive syndrome with psychological and
somatic symptoms. The time and intensity may vary. It may be immediate, delayed, anticipatory, distorted, exaggerated, covered up, or
hidden, but it is real. Each person or family has a unique way of
relating and reacting to change and loss, to crisis and grief. There is no
right or wrong way. We must accept and learn to be comfortable with
the chosen way of the patient to communicate to us that he is hurting;
we must not blame or judge or feel it our duty to alter or suppress the
feelings or behavior of the griever. Pastors and health-care professionals are facilitators in the grief experience, not prescribers or directors. The felt losses of those who grieve are relinquished emotionally
through a process of grief. We do not give up cherished things or persons or important body functions willingly. Adaptation is achieved as
the patient moves through the process of grief, by which, hopefully,
new attachments and goals are formulated.

Comprehensive knowledge and understanding of the basic stages
in the grief process are most helpful, almost essential, to those who
choose to identify with and be supportive of those who sustain severe
losses. Briefly, they are:

(a) Numbness, disbelief, shock, and denial—the "No, not me,"
response. When a person is threatened with great loss, both conscious
and unconscious activity occurs within the individual in an effort to
establish equilibrium. Defenses are established early in life, most of
which are unconscious reactions. At times of severe loss persons do not
deliberately or knowingly maintain a certain behavior. Rather, the ego
is working hard to protect the self in a situation that threatens not only
immediate life situations but perhaps lifelong dreams and goals. It is
well to think of this first response as a healthy protest to a threatening
situation. It is thought that the initial use of denial serves the individual as a delay in which he can garner strength from within to handle the situation. Thus the patient or family responds: "This can't happen to me. I can't believe it. It seems to be a dream. I'll wake up and
find it isn't real," etc. Another aspect of this reaction is seeking evaluations from other professionals. "He's only a resident. What does he
know about cancer (or whatever)?"

(b) Resentment and anger—the "Why me?" response. This stage
can develop into an emotional state of rage, disorganized or explosive
outbursts of aggression, and a lack of control, all of which are difficult
to cope with from the point of view of family and staff. It is displaced

in all directions and projected onto the environment, the staff, the pastor, God, and self. It is a time of intense self-questioning which leads to greater bitterness and deeper resentment. The writer has found that the more determined the patient is to ask "why" questions and insist on answers, the greater the possibility that he will become irrational, out of control—even to the extent of total loss of reality. Questions precipitated by loss and suffering have no easy answers. To encourage the patient at this time to switch from "why" questions to "how" questions can be most helpful. "How am I going to relate to my loss? How will I cope? How can I adjust to being without this body function?"

In his book *Where is God When It Hurts?*, Philip Yancey suggests that the Bible teaches that "response," not "cause," should be the important dimension of emphasis in the tragedies of life. All the way through, the Bible steers from the issue of cause to the issue of response. Pain and loss have become a reality in a patient's life. The big question now is, "What will I *do* about it?" Yancey cites the experience of Job as a prime example of this. God avoids a logical, point-by-point explanation. So clear is the Bible on this point, he says, that we must conclude that the real issue is not "Is God responsible?" but "How should I react now that this terrible thing has happened?" Texts that can be of help in encourging the patient to shift from "Why?" to "How?" are: James 1.2-4, 1 Peter 4:12, 13; 1 Peter 1:6, 7; 2 Corinthians 7:8-11.

(c) Guilt: "It's all my fault;"—the "Why not me?" response. Of all the feelings that are associated with suffering and loss, guilt and remorse can be the most devastating. From early childhood we are conditioned to associate pain with punishment. "Mommy told me not to do it. She says it'll teach me a lesson. When I'm bad, I get hurt." "If only I had been more careful." "If I had been willing to listen to Dad, . . ." "My loss is an act of God." "I don't deserve to live." And the expressions of guilt and remorse keep flowing. They are cruel, destructive, and emotionally paralyzing.

If, in fact, the patient did contribute to his loss through poor judgment or whatever, it is important that he be encouraged to believe that God has promised to forgive and that he choose rationally and deliberately to accept the promise of forgiveness that God has provided. Equally important, he must realize how important it is for him to forgive himself. He should be as willing to forgive himself as God is willing to forgive him.

It is also important and hopefully helpful to explore the patient's feelings with him—his basic beliefs about suffering and pain. Many Christians have been taught and seem to actually believe that God is, or can be, the author of pain, suffering, and loss. We hear such comments as: "If I only knew why He is putting me through this, it would help." Again, "Why?" questions should be replaced as soon as possible with "How?" questions.

It is important at this time for the patient to think through his beliefs about suffering carefully. God is not the author of suffering and loss. This is a dangerous distortion of Bible truth. Sufferers already burdened with the problems of intense pain and loss find their spirits all too often further devastated by concepts which make God responsible for their pain. To believe that He is responsible for suffering is to make Him the author of evil.

The patient must be encouraged to see God as a compassionate and loving Heavenly Father who provides His children with good gifts. Our suffering is not His doing, but the result of our human weaknesses, the result of our existence in an un-ideal and evil world. God can enable us to use suffering to develop His character in us, to strengthen our faith in Him, to increase our awareness of how helpless and hopeless we are without Him, to share with us the bounties of His grace. Pain and loss are no more His doing than are sin and death. God does not exempt His children from their basic humanity and their part in the common lot of human loss and pain.

One more observation might be helpful in understanding those who are experiencing guilt and remorse through loss and pain. These feelings can result in what Kübler-Ross (1969) identifies as "bargaining": "Lord, if you will only make me well and remove this terrible loss, I will dedicate my life to you forever." Most bargains are made with God and are usually kept secret. If the patient should make significant strides in recovery and feel that his prayer was answered, his promises, if not carried out, can lead to more guilt problems in the days ahead. This becomes especially critical if the promises are of such magnitude that it becomes seemingly impossible for the patient to fulfill them. Again, it is important that these feelings be explored and resolved through a proper understanding of God's love and His willingness to understand our human feelings.

One patient, a young girl, went swimming in a spring against the wishes of her father, dived too deeply, and suffered a cervical injury with resulting quadriplegia. Her deep sense of guilt led to profound depression, the next stage in the grief process.

(d) Depression—the "Woe is me" or "Poor me" response. It can be safely said that all patients with physical disability experience moments of real depression at one time or another. It may vary from a state of mild sadness to the extremes of suicide and psychotic delusions. It appears that the degree of depression is less determined by the nature or severity of the loss than by the particular individual who suffers it and the significant meaning the loss has for the patient.

Depression is both a symptom and an adaptation to life experience and can present itself in a variety of ways. In the milder forms the patient is quiet, inhibited, unhappy, self-depreciative, discouraged, and uninterested in surroundings. As the depressive mood deepens there is a constant, unpleasant tension. The patient's interests are very limited and always melancholy. Conversation becomes inhibited. Sleep becomes difficult. Bodily symptoms such as headache, loss of appetite, fatigue, and lack of concentration are more frequent.

Depression is the result of not only a sense of loss, but also a loss of mastery resulting from the disability. Much of our self-esteem is derived from accomplishments that have social value. In the maturing process we learn to walk, to talk, to control our bladders and bowels, to dress ourselves, to wash ourselves, and to perform a host of other activities. When a physical disability strikes, many of these skills and controls are threatened, even lost. The patient is thus projected back into a childlike, helpless state, and this regression leads to depression, particularly if the development of many of these basic skills was associated with traumatic earlier experiences.

Therapeutic strategy in dealing with both guilt and depression must be aimed at helping the patient, or just permitting the patient to label the source of his guilt and depression. We can then help him distinguish between the source and the effect.

Depressed persons also need continual support and assurance of their self-worth, their preciousness as persons, of the value of *being* rather than the value of *doing*. They also need rehabilitation programs that permit them to achieve in areas where they still have great capacity for achievement.

(e) The rational acceptance or coping response. "What now?" "I accept my true condition, the real situation. What are the options? How can I best relate to the changes and losses in my life?"

Since it would be impossible because of the brevity of this chapter to discuss all of these very real stages and responses to grief and severe loss in detail, a careful study of Dr. Kübler-Ross's book entitled *On Death and Dying* is recommended. Kübler-Ross identifies and illustrates these stages of grief. Another good source book in this area is *Symptomatology and Management of Acute Grief* by Erich Lindeman. These basic psychological and somatic components of the grief process are similar in all kinds of severe crisis and loss and should be understood by those who seek to comfort and support grieving persons.

3. *Stress.* Stress is the individual's response to a stressful situation, which in this case is the loss of arms and/or legs or the loss of their function. Stress pervades the total being. It is the person's total self-response to loss, the body's non-specific response to demands created by crises.

Understanding the patient's responses to stress is important to administering effective support. We want to be helpful to those who are experiencing stress, to facilitate in their adaptation to stress. It is helpful for us to be aware of factors inherent in adapting to threat or loss. By understanding and recognizing the level of stress the patient is experiencing, we can better accept aggressive, threatening behavior as a healthy reaction rather than as a personal attack.

There are definitive levels of stress. Obviously, the greater the threat or loss, the greater becomes the stress factor. The first level is what we might call minor stresses of everyday life. These stresses are generally manifested by crying it out, laughing it off, falling asleep, swearing, slips of the tongue, a desire to gain approval or love, somatic discharges such as frequent urination, overeating, increased smoking or drinking. Even these reactions to stress can deplete an individual's energy and reduce his efficiency and pleasure.

The second level of stress results in a partial withdrawal or partial distortion of reality. The patient may faint or have amnesia. The stress symptoms of the first level become more pronounced. Both of these levels, with their symptoms, are generally temporary for the duration of the emergency.

The third level is characterized by disorganized explosive outbursts of aggression, loss of control, and further retreat and detachment from reality. This, if stress continues, results in serious denial and fantasy and can be difficult to handle. Skilled professional help is essential at this level. We must sense, as we relate to persons who are suffering severe stress, when to make referrals and seek the help of those who are highly skilled in relating to severe emotional problems.

Stress management and detection is also a broad and extensive field of study which can only be touched upon here. However, we should be familiar with the basic signals of stress, some of which are: ignoring the facts; missing the details; lack of ability to sleep, to concentrate, to remember; overreaction to almost everything that involves the patient; underestimation of one's own responsibilities; refusal to cooperate; etc. The patient must be encouraged to develop his own awareness of stress, of unsatisfactory behavior and responses which will not contribute to basic solutions to his problem. We, as pastors or counselors, can help the patient to be objective, to think and act from his head rather than from his feelings. We can help him to consider that at such a time of crisis and loss his feelings may not always be accurate. He must be encouraged to dwell on, to concentrate on, the things or assets he still has rather than on those things he no longer has.

The principal enemies of the severely handicapped are fatalism, passivity, and dependence. Fatalism is a state of mind in which the patient concludes that his destiny, his fate, is now totally beyond his control; thus there is nothing he can do to change his situation or condition. In a sense he is being overruled or his life is in the complete control of forces or circumstances beyond his control. "What's to be is to be; I have no control." This leads to passivity—an acceptance of one's predetermined fate without a desire to resist or react to the problem. And this can result in feelings of utter helplessness, a state of being totally dependent upon others for survival. Obviously this is a totally devastating sequence of reactions and feelings.

The patient must have continual access or exposure to positive, genuine encouragement when under severe stress. He must be encouraged to believe that he *can* actively control or influence his destiny and look forward to a life of reasonable self-sufficiency. A positive mental attitude is vital to his recovery and to reducing the level of stress and increasing his ability to cope.

4. *Coping.* Coping is active, cognitive exercise in choosing among alternatives for resolving and adapting to the crisis and loss experience. The counselor can be of tremendous help in encouraging the patient to select a list of alternatives, to utilize all of his previous learning and skills, to consider new and different ways of making his life meaningful and finding fulfillment and happiness in spite of his handicap. This is the reconstruction stage. This process of setting new goals and objectives, taking inventory of what still remains, can take hours of careful support, unconditional commitment, unending devotion, and understanding love. We are all inclined to forget the handicapped when the critical stages of loss and grief are over. This is tragic, for the loss continues to plague them long after they leave the hospital.

It is indeed a rewarding experience to accompany the patient through this process of reorganization and reconstruction, to walk beside him through the acceptance stage, to hear him question "What now?" and begin the constructive pursuit of getting on with his life.

5. *Intellectualism.* This term is used to describe an attempt on the part of the patient to avoid the disturbing impact of loss and the reorganization coping process through mastery of knowledge about the stressor—in this case the paralysis or loss of limb. The patient seems to try to deny his emotional reaction to the loss through extensive reading and research in the area of his handicap. He becomes an "expert" in his own mind. This can become threatening to the nurses and counselors in that he may ask questions for which they may have no fingertip answers. It is a way of gaining recognition and attention, but generally does not contribute much to basic problem solving in terms of adjustment to illness and loss.

6. *Rationalization.* This is an attempt to justify the loss in one way or another. This seems to offer a measure of comfort. The line of thinking, however, may be quite illogical. The patient may say, "It is because I am so strong and have so much faith in God that I have lost my arms or legs." We must be willing to accept, especially in the initial phases of the loss, the feelings of the patient even though these feelings and observations are quite illogical, even erroneous. Perhaps at a later time, if such thinking would persist, we might want to help the patient to see the inaccuracy of his feelings.

In summary of this section on psychological responses, when persons are faced with losses that pose a threat to their ego, their very existence, they will respond in numerous ways. None of these unique, individual responses to the trauma, the tragedy, the grief, and the pain of loss are either right or wrong. They are our psychological adjustment to loss and are important to the final adaptation and reorganization of a precious life. The product of successful grieving is growth. The essential ingredient for successful grieving is an atmosphere of love and concern. Effective facilitators in the grieving experience care with a passion. They believe that a patient and/or family needs individuals around who look and act as if they were trying to understand. The ultimate management of severe loss and change does not occur until after mourning has taken place. This process is considered a psychological necessity, not a weakness or self-indulgence. We must be able to listen to our parishioners, listen to our patients—and by listening permit them to go about their psychological repair.

UNIQUE ADJUSTMENMT PROBLEMS OF THE AMPUTEE

1. *Phantom pain.* Estimates of phantom limb pain vary greatly. Most investigators agree that only a small percentage of amputees

suffer incapacitation and enduring limb pain. Phantom pain is generally described as burning, twisting, cramping, shooting, cyclic pain which is perceived as being in the vicinity of the absent extremity. It is considered a pathological condition, whereas a nonpainful phantom limb is relatively normal following amputation. There appear to be personality correlates to the occurrence of persisting pain in a phantom limb. Persons who are known to dislike and resist change, to be at the rigid end of an "adaptable/rigid" behavioral dimension, seem to have more difficulty with phantom pain. These persons are further described to be compulsively self-reliant. For such individuals, the experience of relative helplessness and the need to rely on others, however loving, is a galling and humiliating experience.

Psychiatric theories tend to relate phantom pain to wish fulfillment resulting from the denial of the loss of the limb. It is believed that the painful phantom limb represents an emotional response to the loss of an important body part that is significant in the patient's relationship with others. Hostile feelings, with resulting guilt, develop toward those with whom the patient identifies the mutilated extremity and also toward those on whom he is dependent and whose rejection he fears. Pain may result as punishment for such hostile and guilty emotions. It is also believed that amputation arouses fantasies and superstitions of personal mutilation or improper disposal which, if not resolved, can lead to repression and phantom limb pain. There is an old wives' tale that pain will result if the severed extremity is buried in a cramped position.

Also, a previous morbid association with another amputee known to the patient, or overemphasis by the patient on the value of body parts can produce phantom pain. Permitting the patient to verbalize the meaning for him of the limb or limbs which he has lost, to understand the nature of their disposition and the meaning of such disposition to the patient, with appropriate support for the working through of the process of loss, might prevent, in some cases, the occurrence of phantom limb pain.

2. *Sexual dysfunction and adjustment.* Those of us in pastoral and health care professions who have occasion to relate in a supportive way to amputee or paralysis patients have been reluctant to include sexual problems in our discussion with patients. It is also rare that the patient will spontaneously imply that he or she is having problems or will ask direct questions about such problems. It is only recently that health professionals have become sensitized to the extent that some attention is given to the physiological and psychological problems of sex following amputation or paralysis.

What are some of the sex problems that patients generally face following amputation or paralysis? There is the obvious emotional trauma, the depression and mourning period, the distortion of body image, and the perception of self as not whole, or as ugly, or as no longer feminine or masculine. All of these or any one of these could emotionally affect the sex life of the patient and his spouse. Phantom pain, which we have already discussed, can also be most disturbing—even disastrous—in the performance of the sex act.

Another area of vital concern is the mechanics of body positioning. Balance and movement, or lack of either, may become a real problem. Many of these mechanical problems can be solved by simple alternatives and alterations in position, by encouraging the couple to pursue a second honeymoon in exploration and genuine sharing of their feelings, needs, and satisfactions.

We must be aware of distinctions among sex drive, sex acts, and sexuality. Although a disability may impose alterations in sex acts, the sex drive and sexuality remain intact. Most of the physiological sexual responses seen in the able-bodied remain even in spinal-cord-injured patients. Before meaningful initiation of treatment and direction, the therapist or counselor should know both the patient and spouse as people whose sexuality and sexual function have been shaped by previous specific experiences, attitudes, and beliefs. There are many types of sexual gratification. It may be helpful to encourage the couple to explore and consider sexual activities they would not have considered acceptable previous to the handicap. The couple should be encouraged to freely share their feelings in exploration and sex gratification, and to accept the limitations expressed by such feelings.

THE REHABILITATION STAGE

We come now to the final stage in the experience of the amputee or paralysis patient—that state of being a handicapped person. This is the stage of rehabilitation, of learning to live the remainder of his life with paralyzed limbs or some kind of prosthesis. It is very real. It is loneliness and rejection. It is frustration. The loss never goes away even though most people will have a tendency to adjust to it. It is for the rest of the person's life with no possibility of change.

It would be well for us to picture ourselves in such a state, to try to imagine the experience of such a loss, if we are to be effective in providing long-term support and ministry. We must not forget these dear ones as they leave the hospital. Continual encouragement, reinforcement of self-worth, assistance in setting new goals and objectives, and support in reaching them can determine to a great extent the progress of rehabilitation.

A caring pastor will keep in touch, will assist in every way possible to help the disabled person cope with his disability in every way in which he is capable in his own environment. It would be well for every pastor to explore ways to consistently minister to the needs of the handicapped and suffering with his church board. The possibilities are endless for the pastor who desires to show that he and his church really care: phone calls; personal visitation; assigning well-chosen deacons and elders to keep in touch and report periodically on their contacts; selecting special committees to care for the handicapped and assist them in their daily needs; soliciting the help of local agencies; providing group sessions where persons with similar losses can get together and share their common feelings of frustration, anger, guilt, accomplishment, etc.; providing cassettes of the weekly services of the church and other messages which are available to encourage and provide direction in areas of special need; or special dinners and get-togethers just for the handicapped in the homes of members. Pastors and church members alike are so busy with so many details and responsibilities that it is easy to forget unless special effort is made to remember.

Unless the patient receives tangible rewards and satisfactions in his pursuit of a new way of life, he can easily become discouraged and despondent. Reaffirmation of rehabilitation goals can be encouraged from both the pastor and the membership of the church. Through this display of loving helpfulness and consistent concern, the patient's shattered faith in God can begin to be reestablished. He may also choose to become involved in the activities of the church. This involvement in the years to come can keep him close to those who really care and can continue to provide the spiritual support so necessary for successful rehabilitation and meaningful fulfillment.

THE MINISTRY OF HOPE

"Pastor, is there any hope?" How many times we have been asked this question in moments of despair, when there doesn't seem to be a ghost of a chance of anything good resulting from a devastating accident or a surgeon's report. Pastors are ministers of hope. Hope we must if we are to courageously and meaningfully relate to tragic loss. We cannot survive without the ministry of hope. It is the essential dimension of living that keeps us dreaming, planning, building, adjusting, and coping. It is at the very heart of living. Perhaps this is included in what the Apostle Paul meant when he wrote to the Roman church, "We are saved by hope."

Hope is relational, not circumstantial. It is the result of being able to depend upon the relationships of loving, caring persons. Untold millions of severely handicapped persons have worked their way through the valleys of despair and grief to the mountain tops of success, of glorious fulfillment, because a pastor, a friend, a loved one provided hope.

Ministers of hope will also provide an atmosphere in which hurting persons can eventually see through their tears to the outstretched arms of Jesus. This may take many weeks, even months, but it is most rewarding when it happens.

Every pastor ought to have access to a list of promises to share with those who are hurting. Space will not permit enumerating them all. One that the author often uses is Philippians 4:6, 7: "Don't worry about anything; instead, pray about everything; tell God your needs and don't forget to thank Him for His answers. If you do this you will experience God's peace, which is far more wonderful than the human mind can understand. His peace will keep your thoughts and your hearts quiet and at rest as you trust in Christ Jesus" (Living New Testament). Other promises which contain some of God's greatest gifts for troubled hearts are: Exodus 33:15, "My presence shall go with thee and I will give thee rest"; Deuteronomy 33:25, "As thy days, so shall thy strength be"; Deuteronomy 33:27, "The Almighty God is thy refuge and underneath are the everlasting arms." The Psalms are full of marvelous promises. Among them are: "God is my refuge and strength, a very present help in trouble" Psalm 46:1; "Call upon me in the day of trouble: I will deliver thee, and thou shalt glorify me" Psalm 50:15; "Cast thy burden upon the Lord and He shall sustain thee" Psalm 55:22. Isaiah has provided us with another group of promises that are most encouraging, such as Isaiah 41:10; 43:1, 2; 53:4; and 66:13.

As ministers of hope we must teach the suffering in our midst how to pray, how to claim the promises of God. They must know that

> amid the anthems of the celestial choir, God hears the cries of the weakest human being. We pour out our heart's desire in our closets, we breathe a prayer as we walk by the way, and our words reach the throne of the Monarch of the universe. They may be inaudible to any human ear, but they cannot die away into silence, nor can they be lost through the activities of business that are going on. Nothing can drown the soul's desire (White, *Christ's Object Lessons*, p. 174).

As ministers of hope we must instill faith and trust.

Nothing is apparently more helpless, yet really more invincible than the soul that feels its nothingness and relies wholly on the merits of the Saviour. By prayer, by the study of His word, by faith in His abiding presence, the weakest of human beings may live in contact with the living Christ, and He will hold them by a hand that will never let go (White, *Ministry of Healing*, p. 182).

As ministers of hope we must keep before patients the personal ministry of Jesus, who

. . . came to this world as the unwearied servant of man's necessities. He "took our infirmities, and bare our sicknesses," that He might minister to every need of humanity. The burden of disease and wretchedness and sin He came to remove. It was his mission to bring to men complete restoration; He came to give them health and peace and perfection of character.

Varied were the circumstances and needs of those who besought His aid, and none who came to Him went away unhelped. From Him flowed a stream of healing power, and in body and mind and soul men were made whole (White, *Ministry of Healing*, p. 17).

Hope is further the result of a combination of will power and Divine power, of choice and trust. The combination is invincible. As ministers of hope we must not only show hurting persons how to trust in God, but we must teach them to use their God-given ability to make rational choices and to follow through.

When we, as ministers of hope, choose to experience the hardest and most painful moments in the lives of our people, especially in those who suffer, we are also privileged to see and experience their growth in self-worth and self-confidence, their increase in faith and trust in God, and their increasing ability to successfully meet the crises of life. Thus we experience also the glory of their finest moments.

SUMMARY

When an individual is faced with an event which poses a threat to his self-image, or the loss of a valued body part or function, he will respond with a variety of coping and defensive behaviors. His behavior will be disorganized and he will experience somatic and psychological difficulties for a time. The level of the stress that the individual experiences is reflected in his observable behavior. Supportive intervention during this time of crisis can facilitate a healthy resolution of the problem with possible growth of the individual's future coping capacities and abilities.

The strategies of our supportive ministry which we make available to the individual in crisis and loss must consider his psychological resources and capabilities, his cognitive mastery of the situation that enables him to make workable choices, his capacities or skills in meeting changes and demands, and his religious value system which can provide inner strength and spiritual support.

One final point of observation, reemphasis, and challenge. We have noted that losses during a person's life destroy identity by separating the patient from things, persons, body parts and functions. Grief, we have observed, is the patient's total response to losses which require the traumatic experiences of "having to let go of" and "having to take on." In this process the patient is forced to move from (1) an identifiable somebody, to (2) an identifiable nobody, to (3) an identifiable somebody else. To move from (1) to (3) we pass through the valley of "nobodyness." Persons cannot tolerate this feeling of "nobodyness" for long without the danger of severe emotional problems. The feeling of "nobodyness" can be greatly diminished by your consistent concern and understanding support as a pastor and friend. You can also, through your contact with other family members, hospital staff, and friends, organize and encourage an identity support system around the patient that can very possibly determine the rate and extent of recovery and rehabilitation. You, friend, are an important person to that amputee or paralysis patient. God's blessing to you as you, with His help, fulfill your important assignment!

BIBLIOGRAPHY

Bitter, James A. *Introduction to Rehabilitation.* St. Louis, Mo.: C. V. Mosby Co., 1979.

Cummings, Victor. "Amputees and Sexual Dysfunction." *Archives of Physical Medicine and Rehabilitation,* January 1975.

Frazier, C. F., and Kolb, L. C. "Psychiatric Aspects of the Phantom Limb." *Orthopedic Clinic of North America* 1 (1970): 481-495.

Frazier, Claude A. *Healing and Religious Faith.* Philadelphia: United Press, 1974.

Freedmann, L. A., and Freedman, L. "The Quality of Hope for the Amputee." *Archives of Surgery,* June 1975.

Garrison, John. "Stress Management Training for the Handicapped." *Archives of Physical Medicine and Rehabilitation,* December 1978.

Kolb, L. C. *The Painful Phantom: Psychology, Physiology and Treatment.* Springfield, Ill.: Charles C. Thomas, 1954.

Kübler-Ross, Elisabeth. *On Death and Dying.* New York: Macmillan, 1969.

Kvaraceus, William C., and Hayes, E. Nelson. *If Your Child is Handicapped.* Boston: Porter Sargent, Publisher, 1969.

LaHaye, Tim F. *How to Win Over Depression.* New York: Zondervan Corp., 1974.

Lawson, Norman C. "Significant Events in the Rehabilitation Process." *Archives of Physical Medicine and Rehabilitation,* December 1978.

Lindeman, Erich. "Symptomatology and Management of Acute Grief." In *Beyond Grief: Studies in Crisis Intervention.* New York: J. Aronson, Inc., 1979.

McDonald, Eugene T. *Understand Those Feelings.* Pittsburgh: Stanwix House, 1962.

Moos, Rudolph. *Coping with Physical Illness.* New York: Plenum Medical Book Co., 1977.

Parkes, C. M. "Factors Determining the Persistence of Phantom Pain in the Amputee." *Journal of Psychosomatic Research* 17 (1973): 87-108.

Roberts, Sharon L. *Behavioral Concepts and the Critically Ill Patient.* Englewood Cliffs, N.J.: Prentice-Hall, Inc., 1976.

Sandough, Leshner, and Fino. "Sexual Adjustment in the Chronically Ill and Physically Disabled." *Archives of Physical Medicine and Rehabilitation,* July 1972.

Schaeffer, Edith. *Affliction.* Old Tappan, N.J.: Fleming H. Revell, 1973.

Spencer, W. A. "Is Anybody Listening?" *Archives of Physical Medicine and Rehabilitation,* May 1970.

Stryker, Ruth. *Rehabilitative Aspects of Acute and Chronic Nursing Care.* Philadelphia: W. B. Saunders, 1977.

Tournier, Paul. *Guilt and Grace.* New York: Harper and Row, 1958.

Tournier, Paul. *The Healing of Persons.* New York: Harper and Row, 1965.

White, Ellen G. *Christ's Object Lessons.* Washington: Review and Herald Publishing Association, 1941.

White, Ellen G. *The Ministry of Healing.* Mountain View, Calif.: Pacific Press Publishing Association, 1942.

Wright, B. *Physical Disability—A Psychological Approach.* New York: Harper and Row, 1960.

Yancy, Phillip. *Where Is God When It Hurts?* Grand Rapids, Mich.: Zondervan Corp., 1977.

Yuker, H. E., Block, J. R., and Young, J. H. "The Measurement of Attitudes Toward Disabled Persons." New York: Research Council Bulletin 55, 1955.

John Treolo

9

Pastoral Care of the Visually Handicapped

A favorite occasion for church members of any denomination is potluck meals. Whether following church services or during social gatherings, potlucks bring congregations together. A spirit of unity and fellowship permeates such events. Blind members are welcomed here also, aren't they?

One blind lady from New York discovered a repugnant "welcome" from her church colleagues at one such gathering. She was a newly baptized church member, attending one of her first potlucks. Wanting to participate and at the same time make a good impression on her sighted associates, she meticulously prepared a macaroni and cheese casserole as part of her contribution. As the festive occasion began and members flocked to the serving line, she, out of courtesy or to avoid embarrassment for herself, went to the end of the line. Approaching the casserole section, she noticed her dish remained untouched. She was puzzled.

During the clean-up period, she overheard two "saints" talking. To her surprise their discussion centered around who had prepared the casserole that no one ate. The new blind member took her still-untouched casserole home following that potluck. She was crushed. Wouldn't you be?

Several questions arise from this incident. Do blind persons cook that badly? Does their inability to see imply that their cooking utensils are repulsive? Can we shove the blame for this incident on the pastor's shoulders? Is it his job to tell the sighted members that the visually-impaired can very often cook as well as they? Or are church members just that insensitive to the feelings of blind persons? These and other questions will be discussed in this chapter.

Give anyone a choice of handicaps and nine out of ten times blindness will be placed at the bottom of the list. We tarry in a majestic, colorful world. God loves a variety of assorted hues. Evidence of His colorful, creative ability exists in the people He formed; this fact also is inherent in His second book, nature, and in many other visual testimonies. Our world and much of our dependence on it are visual. Some experts have concluded that mankind comprehends some eighty percent of learned behavior through sight.

Where does this leave those who have been deprived of this precious sense? Before addressing the clergy specifically, let's take a layman's look at blindness.

IN THE BEGINNING . . .

Blindness is nothing new to this sin-cursed society. Prior to the birth of our Saviour, blind people were found everywhere. In ancient times blind persons were shunned and neglected. Their only livelihood was begging for alms or crumbs from humanitarian citizens.

But God hadn't planned it this way. In His original design for earth and man, handicaps were nonexistent. Genesis 1:26, 27 states, "Then God said, 'Let us make man in our image, according to our likeness;' . . . so God created man in His own image." Since God Himself was perfect, He intended for the people He created in His own image to be in a similar state. We find no records in the first book of the Bible pertaining to birth defects. Moses, the first historian, presents a clear picture of social life in the beginning of the earth's history, but we find no traces of anyone born blind, deaf, crippled, or imbecilic, and no report of a natural death in infancy or childhood. In fact, the average life span before the Flood was nearly a thousand years, and cases of children dying before their parents were so extraordinary that Moses specifically mentions one in Genesis 11:28: "And Haran died in the presence of his father Terah, in the land of his brethren."

There are numerous cases of blindness found later in the Scriptures. One of the earliest accounts of blindness is found in the giving of the ceremonial birthright from the prophet Isaac to his eldest son, Esau. "And it came to pass that when Isaac was old, and his eyes were dim, so that he could not see, he called Esau his eldest son . . ." Genesis 27:1. Realizing his father's sight loss, Jacob, the younger of the two sons, intercepted the birthright that rightfully belonged to Esau.

Our Supreme Example Himself was very sympathetic during His earthly ministry to those without physical sight. On no less than twelve different occasions do the Gospel writers record that Christ restored sight to the blind, displaying His great compassion to this class. Matthew 12:22 reads, "Then was brought unto Him one possessed with a devil, blind, and dumb: and He healed him, insomuch that the blind and dumb spoke and saw." These biblical miracles were no accident. Christ knew that for the blind to believe in Him, He would have to remove their physical affliction first, thus opening their eyes to accept the salvation He came to offer.

For others, to show what direction God wanted them to go, blindness was imparted. Paul, formerly Saul of Tarsus, persecutor of Christians, authored more than half the books found in the New Testament, but not before he was blinded and converted on the road to Damascus. "And he was three days without sight . . . And immediately there fell from his eyes as it had been scales: and he received sight forthwith and arose, and was baptized" Acts 9:9, 18. Besides Christ, no one in the New Testament did more for the early Christian church than Paul. But the "light that shined on him from heaven" (Acts 9:3), blinding him and leading to his tremendous conversion, is believed to have harmed Paul's eyesight. He later details what many believe to be his own physical sight problem in 2 Corinthians 12:7: ". . . there was given to me a thorn in the flesh . . ." Even champions of God are not exempt from physical problems.

WHERE WE ARE NOW . . .

Moving from biblical history to modern times we see quite a contrast: no longer is there a Man capable of restoring eyesight by a simple command; no longer is begging for alms a lucrative occupation for the blind; no longer can the blind rely upon their blindness as a crutch to help them survive in a sighted world. The estimated forty to eighty million blind persons currently living in the twentieth century have progressed a long way from the falsehoods and stereotypes that plagued the blind not more than a few hundred years ago.

Frances A. Koestler, in her excellent book on the social history of blindness, *The Unseen Minority*, describes the blind of times past:

They [the blind] were feared, shunned, pitied, ignored. Some were thought to be blessed with magical powers, others to be accursed for their sins. They were princes and beggars, bards and soothsayers, storytellers and buffoons. Some were killed as infants, others were tolerated in youth but abandoned to die by the roadside or even buried alive when they grew old and infirm. . . . There were others who never in their lives ventured from home and hearthside. . . . some were thrown into madhouses, pesthouses, almshouses, where they could be kept out of public view . . .

Not a very pretty picture of the way things used to be for the blind, is it? But just how far has our modern society come? Helen Keller, both blind and deaf, forerunner in implementing social programs and helps for the blind in the mid-1920s, once said, "The greatest problem facing blind persons is not their blindness, but the lack of vision of their sighted friends." This lack of vision that Miss Keller spoke about over fifty years ago is still prevalent in our current society. The blind are still misunderstood and pitied, and are welcomed into the average sighted person's home just one notch ahead of the Hong Kong flu.

BLINDNESS

What is blindness? Close your eyes tightly for a moment. This is blindness. Imagine waking up to meet each new day in this state; imagine groping and stumbling in unfamiliar surroundings; imagine depending on friends or taxi service for appointments not within walking distance. Now open your imagination and your eyes and appreciate your sighted existence.

There are various forms of blindness. Some are totally blind, unable to see their surroundings, though they may possess light perception; others are legally blind, who, although classified as blind, have some vision, but have visual measurements of 20/200 or worse in both eyes; still others, labeled as partially sighted, have sight better than 20/200 but still have difficulty seeing. Then there are those who are blind in just one eye but may eventually go totally blind due to the immense pressure on the remaining good eye.

Glaucoma causes still another type of blindness. Generally affecting those past thirty-five, glaucoma is a progressive eye disease associated with too much pressure within the eye. This pressure reduces the blood supply to the retina, which is a vital link in the seeing process, progressively destroying nerve cells. Glaucoma is unpreventable. The blindness it causes, however, is not. If the disease is detected in its early stages and properly treated, the damage already done, although irreversible, can be prevented from spreading and doing further harm. Persons past thirty-five should have a regular eye examination every two years. It is estimated that one million persons currently are afflicted wth glaucoma and do not know it!

Compared to the total population of blind persons worldwide, the United States has a relatively small number. There are some six million legally blind Americans; 500,000 are totally blind in this country. An estimated 50,000 persons will lose their sight this year.

Many are born blind; others acquire blindness through accidental means or wars, still others through recklessness or carelessness. One elderly lady lost her eyesight when her husband of some forty years went into a state of drunken rage and struck her eye with a sharp object. She is now nearly totally blind. A newborn infant was blinded when his mother cut out his eyes with a razor blade. The mother's reason: she couldn't stand to hear her son cry anymore!

Medical science has done much to decrease the amount of blindness found in newborn infants. In the 1940s and early '50s some twelve thousand babies lost their sight shortly after birth and no one knew why. Termed retrolental fibroplasia, which means a fibrous growth behind the eye's crystalline lens, the mystery was finally solved when it was discovered that each new case had a common clue: all babies had a premature birth. Sustaining the life of a premature infant forty years ago required adding pure oxygen to the incubator. This process did indeed save many lives, but it was later discovered that oxygen in its purest state burned undeveloped tissue. Unfortunately for many newborn babies, their retinas were usually undeveloped, resulting in instant and, more often than not, permanent blindness. Nurses concerned about breathing complications of the newborn had no idea that the oxygen they added to the incubator destroyed the sight of many infants.

Being born blind has some advantages: one becomes accustomed to a state of darkness; the psychological depression of losing one's sight at a later age is nonexistent. It is far easier for one who loses his sight early in life to learn to read braille, the universally accepted alphabet for the blind, than it is for those who lose their sight later in life.

There are disadvantages, however, for those who have never seen. How would you explain a sunset, a soaring eagle gracefully gliding through the air, or a simple color photograph to one who has never visually seen? Unless a blind person can feel an object or have a vivid descriptive picture painted for him, perceiving the object or subject may be impossible. As one blind, well-adjusted man puts it, "Blindness is like a dead-end street. When you come to a dead end, you must find another route. The same with blindness. You must work around the inconvenience you face daily."

Many sight-impaired persons develop "blindisms" at a young age and often retain these into adulthood. Blindisms are habits which are usually perceived as abnormal by the sighted world. These include rocking or swaying constantly when talking, sitting, or standing; jumping up and down when excited; using one's fingers excessively; or talking to one's self even when people are nearby. For many blind people these gestures are simply learned behavior. Either overprotective parents or sighted associates fearful of hurting the blind person's feelings have allowed the child to consider these habits as normal. These blindisms are very distressing to sighted people and very often present a barrier to communication and fellowship. One sixteen-year-old blind boy would feel the face of the person he was talking to. Perhaps this is why some sighted persons perceive the blind as being weird! Talking frankly, yet tactfully, with a blind person about personal appearance or blindisms is advisable.

It is imperative for the blind to be independent. Independent mobility, whether by cane or guide dog, lets the sighted world know that the blind person desires independence, and this, in turn, will result in a sense of respect from the sighted community. We all need some sort of independence and the blind are no exception. One blind lady daily walks some fourteen blocks to work, crossing two very congested intersections. She insists on walking, thus helping her independence. During inclement weather, of course, sighted assistance is mandatory.

Living independently is preferred by most sight-impaired persons. Many blind people do an excellent job of cooking and housekeeping. But just as some sighted individuals tend to be a bit lazy, some blind people do also. Be helpful in any way you can, but do not overdo it. Make sure the blind person keeps his independence and that you are not burdened by too many requests. The visually impaired, like anyone else, know a "gift horse" when they see one and sometimes try to take advantage of such generosity. Be helpful, yet firm and tactful.

Jim Walker, professional counselor at the Nebraska Division of Rehabilitation for the Visually Impaired, comments on the way he counsels the blind:

> My need for sensitivity must be individualized. I do not counsel
> a blind person any differently than I do a sighted person. I must talk
> common sense first and foremost. If one has just lost his sight, I con-
> sistently push that life is not a tragedy, that blindness is not a world of

darkness. Of course, the sighted public tends to assert this stereotype upon the visually impaired. I always assert myself by emphasizing that blind persons are first-class citizens and that blindness is reduced to a nuisance level.

Mr. Walker, who received his degree in sociology from the University of Michigan, speaks from a two-fold experience: he is a trained counselor and is blind himself.

WHAT THE PASTOR'S ROLE SHOULD BE

As pastor, your calling is to minister to your congregation and your community. When there is a need among your parishioners, you are there to help—any time, any place. The same should hold true for blind members. But there are a few exceptions that need to be emphasized.

Greeting a blind person at the church's front door each week should not be any different from greeting anyone else. The exceptions start after the warm welcome. Sighted members are handed a church bulletin detailing the morning's program—sermon title, opening song, scriptural texts, and special features, in addition to special announcements not emphasized from the pulpit. Blind members have to either ask someone to read the bulletin or listen intently and hope to hear all they need to know.

Since brailling the weekly bulletins may be asking too much for the average pastor or church member, what about recording the program and weekly announcements and then circulating this tape to blind members a day or two prior to church services? This would be a welcomed benefit and just might encourage other blind persons to attend your church. Another innovative concept suggested by one pastor of twenty-two years is to implement a Code-a-Phone system. When dialed, it would present a five-minute message highlighting not only church activities but interesting happenings in the community.

Transportation to and from church is often perplexing to the blind, especially during inclement weather or for those who are not within walking distance of the sanctuary. Many churches have vans that could transport the visually impaired or other handicapped individuals to church and perhaps members could share in this responsibility. It might be beneficial to divide the responsibility among many persons so that more people could share the blessings of helping others.

We learn as children that talking during services is taboo. For the blind, however, some talking is necessary. They would surely miss a large portion of the service if someone with sight did not whisper what is taking place. Perhaps a special section of the church could be set aside for this purpose.

Dr. Jack Bohannon, then senior pastor of a two-thousand-member church with at least a half dozen sight-impaired members, offers some helpful counsel to fellow clergy:

> I treat blind persons psychologically like anyone else. Their sight loss is the only handicap they possess; the function of the mind is still very keen. Their spiritual problems are usually very similar to those of sighted persons. I do recognize their need for transportation and becoming familiar with the church plant. I'm very sensitive about embarrassing anyone, especially the visually impaired. Most are able to move about and be independent once they become familiar with the design of the church.

As leader of your "flock," you may have to set the example for your sighted members. If you make the blind feel welcome at church, including them in social gatherings, inviting them to your house for dinner, chances are your sighted members will follow this pattern.

According to Bill Moors, who most recently worked in an unofficial pastoral capacity to the estimated 45,000 blind persons in metropolitan New York City, the pastor must take the initiative in bridging the gap between his sighted and blind members. Moors cites one example: "I've seen blind people go to a church and stand in the foyer for twenty or thirty minutes before the pastor himself had to assist the blind person to his seat. Everyone else just walked by. It was obvious he was blind because of his guide dog standing nearby." Moors goes on to state that very often the pastor himself will be uneasy around the blind and this uneasiness is obvious to both sighted and blind members. The key word, Moors insists, is interaction. Interaction must take place for the close fellowship we all need in a religious setting.

Most feel the blind persons themselves must take the initiative to "break the ice," so to speak. Walker, the blind counselor previously mentioned, cites a personal experience.

> About a year ago the church I attend held a traditional Christmas service where members are handed candles as they enter the sanctuary. As the service closes, the lights are dimmed and the members depart with lit candles, signifying turning the darkness into light. My wife, sister-in-law, her husband, and I were not given candles as we entered that night. I spoke to the minister afterwards and he thought we had chosen not to participate. Obviously, I wanted to speak to the usher at the door to correct this impression.

But I had to take the initiative or this type of practice might have continued.

Blind persons, like others, like to participate in church activities. Music is an area where many blind people excel; talking and sharing their love for Christ are other areas. Imagine the benefits to our "church leaders of tomorrow" if a blind person were appointed to assist with the children's division. What better person to talk about Christ's compassion and love than someone with adversity who has had to accept His grace?

The last few examples about the blind taking the initiative refer, obviously, to church members. But what about the non-church-member? Just how important is religion to the blind?

Jerry Regler, principal of the Nebraska School for the Visually Handicapped, comments:

> I can't say that it is any different from people in general. I think a human being has a need for faith and religion. If someone doesn't guide him along that path, he'll make up his own. There is a tendency by some blind people to blame God for their sight loss and, unless someone explains it differently, they may go their entire lives blaming God.
>
> The church as a social community can be quite important to the blind. It's healthy to be with other people with similar beliefs, ethics, and morals. The social function may be the drawing card at first until the visually-impaired understand the immense needs of the religious aspect.

Moors, on the other hand, believes religion is not only important for the blind person to achieve a well-rounded life, but essential as well.

> I think it's extremely important, but you must treat each case individually. If a blind man has an emotional problem, I must deal with that first before I can speak to him about religious matters. It takes patience and a lot of hard work but the end results are worth it. I try to ask myself, "How important is a person won to Christ?" Then I think of all Christ has done for me, and it seems like ministering to the blind is not that difficult after all.

Ministers, Moors explains, can do a great deal to help the blind not only hear but "see" the sermon each week.

> Pastors should use descriptive illustrations while preaching. I'm not referring to using a child's language, but neither would I advise talking like a Ph.D. Even examples or illustrations that seem so clear

to us may not be understood by the blind. We need to use illustrations that are relevant to those without sight, concepts that are real to the visually-impaired person.

IN THEIR OWN WORDS

This chapter would not be complete without hearing from the class we are addressing, principally the blind and visually impaired. We could discuss theory and the psychology of the blind endlessly, but unless we let the blind speak for themselves we have missed a crucial point. The next section will be devoted to personal interviews with six blind persons. They were asked to comment on various issues pertaining to God, religion, the church, and how they would like to be treated by sighted clergy and members. Fictitious first names have been used for reasons of anonymity. This writer appreciates their frankness and sincerity in trying to help both sighted pastors and church members alike to understand them better.

Fred: *I joined one church where I perceived the members as thinking, "Well, we have him in the church but what do we do with him now? We can't restore his sight. And since we can't restore his sight, this seems to be a pretty hopeless proposition."*

This is where I think pastoral counseling tends to be its weakest. Many feel that blindness is the end of the world. I've run into this reaction from clergy of all faiths. On the other side of the coin, I've seen the pastor who always answers, "Don't worry about your blindness now because in heaven you will be able to see again." This, of course, does not give much practical encouragement to us here on earth, does it? It is especially difficult to the newly blinded individual who may have thirty or forty years before he dies. I'm not arguing with the pastor's theology; I'm more concerned with his common sense. What the minister should say is, "Hey, this isn't the end of the world. Maybe this is a new beginning, a new challenge, a new opportunity to do, not necessarily the same things, but different things."

Ministers will be the ones who set the example one way or the other. Most of the sighted members will look to the minister for advice and follow his pattern. I'd like to encourage both ministers and sighted members to adhere to the old Indian adage, "Let me judge no man till I walk two weeks in his moccasins." In other words, treat us (the blind) as you expect to be treated. But don't overdo the pity or sympathy. Let us empathize with one another together. And by God's grace we will be as one.

There is one burden I'd like to share with ministers reading this chapter. In counseling prior to marriage, ministers must realize that blind persons have the same biological, spiritual, and psychological needs as everybody else. As ministers, you should be aware that most well-adjusted blind people will someday marry. Pastors should also know that just because one spouse or the couple are blind, this does not imply that their offspring will be born sightless. This is one area that is often overlooked in a chapter of this nature.

Julie: *I've been a Christian all my life. As a youngster, I felt I was treated like the "little blind girl." At twenty-seven, I still feel that even today. Sighted members are still hesitant to relate to me. Other members seem hard-pressed to get into a deep conversation with me, maybe because they feel I can't think for myself. I deeply feel ministers have a grave responsibility to let their parishioners know that handicapped people are just as much a part of their churches as anyone else. I prefer to be considered an equal person rather than "this handicapped person."*

I think a personal visit from a pastor is very important to the sight-impaired. In the quietness of his home, the blind person has opportunity to explain more about his handicap to the pastor, helping him become more at ease, and, in turn, the minister could convey this openness to his sighted members. This personal visit also lets the blind person know the pastor is interested in him and is not avoiding his home just because he's blind.

We all have needs in life; blind people are no exception. A minister should find out what these needs are and try to find workable solutions and helps for the same. I feel it's very important for me to participate during services. This way I know I'm part of the church and not just sitting in the pews week after week being useless. I encourage every pastor to let the blind become involved. Many uninvolved sighted members could learn a good lesson from someone whom they may consider "inferior" or "less talented."

Arthur: *I've been interested in the Bible since I was a kid, so the logical profession for me was to be a minister. My professors in college didn't discourage me from becoming a pastor; but when I entered the seminary, a few did suggest alternate work. I know my handicap kept me from working in this profession. I currently do volunteer pastoring and counseling. Through the years most sighted members have related to me quite well, probably out of amazement more than anything else.*

They were awed that a blind person could excel in life.

My advice to pastors is to be open with blind members. Try to learn all you can about the individual and his handicap. Utilize his good points and try to improve on the bad. If a minister feels comfortable relating to people, he needn't feel uncomfortable relating to a blind person. But I do realize that most people, pastors and laymen alike, have the concept that blindness is a terrible thing and they are at a loss to know what to do.

A pastor not knowing what to do should be honest and say, "I'm not acquainted with your handicap. Could you help me see if there's any way in which I could be of help to you and, if there's not, what I could do for you otherwise?" Of course, one can go to the opposite extreme in trying to be helpful. One day at college I was on my way to the library, a route I had traveled many times. A humanitarian student came running to me and practically picked me up bodily trying to assist me to my destination. I told him thanks but I was heading in the right direction. I would never attempt to fault anyone for attempting to help.

Michelle: *I feel a big factor lies on the blind person's shoulders. If we project a helpless image or one that is desiring or demanding sympathy, we will be treated that way. If we take the initiative to lend our support through music or reading scriptures whenever possible, I think we will be treated like anyone else. I tend to be a bit more patient with a newly blinded person. He doesn't need sympathy either, but rather companionship and friendship to help him overcome any depression or oppression he may be feeling.*

I was fortunate when I became an active member of my church. I was warmly welcomed into fellowship. If there was something I did not understand about church doctrine or standards, I wasn't harshly reprimanded, but rather told, "Perhaps you should pray about that." I was told in a tactful way that this was something I should consider seriously.

I try not to dwell so much on how I'm treated as on how I involve myself. I do concede that the pastor must set the example and should pass this attitude of concern to his successor as well.

When I'm sitting in church I like to know what's going on. I don't feel it's too disruptive for the person near me to whisper a verbal description of some of the highlights of the service. In fact, I always ask the person near me, "Who's sitting on my right?" This way I know who is there and I can be courteous when passing the offering plate or asking for a verbal description. I try not to take the initiative, however.

Without the person acknowledging himself first, it's difficult to know who is sitting next to me. A sighted person can tell by a smile if the person wants to be communicative. It's hard to tell by a whisper. I would surely welcome a "Hi, I'm Sally Rogers; how are you today?"

I would encourage a pastor never to say from the pulpit, "We all know we have a blind person present today and let's all be friendly." This is very stereotypic.

Roger: *My vocal ability and communication skills during personal testimonies have broken the ice for many sighted church members. I guess you could say I'm treated as kind of a novelty item. I would still insist the pastor take the initiative, assess the needs of the blind members, and make them feel comfortable. I would also encourage the pastor to make contact with sighted members who may be able to involve the blind in other church activities.*

I do feel a bit left out not knowing what the program is from week to week without hearing some announcement from the front. Since the blind give their offerings each week, which are earmarked for bulletins and other xeroxed material, I don't feel it's asking too much to have these same materials recorded for those who cannot see to read. If this is too costly, I would not insist on the church making an exception just for me. But it would be most helpful to know what is happening in my church.

I enjoy the fellowship, not only during services but after church as well. I like to meet and converse with people. God is real to me; He's perfect. Unfortunately, we live in a world less than perfect, and it's this world I must contend with in order to be ready for the ecstasy of heaven.

Sharon: *At times I feel many ministers feel uncomfortable near me and they ignore or evade me during church each week. The same must be said of many sighted members. Sometimes I sit in church and I wish someone would tell me what's going on up front or just read the bulletin to me. They don't seem to think of it and I guess I'm just too proud to ask. Sometimes I don't even know who's talking up front unless I recognize a voice. I know I should take the initiative also, but I just hate to be a burden. It would be so much easier if someone would offer assistance.*

There's a blind couple in my church who stopped attending simply because no one paid any attention to them. And you know, that's sad. We are all God's children. We are equal in His eyes. Sometimes my sight problem does bother me, but it's more of an inconvenience than anything else. I'm so thankful God accepts me as I am.

Differing opinions, but all with the same message: accept the blind as they are; be helpful but not sympathetic; involve them but do not embarrass them; and treat them as equal members in your church.

IN CLOSING

There are several other ways in which ministers can assist the visually impaired members in their congregations. Your blind members are eligible to receive free materials from the state where you reside. Each state, through both federal and state funding, supplies reading materials, cassettes, talking-book players, and many other helpful items for the blind. Services include braille, large-print, and recorded magazines and books covering almost every subject from religion to mystery to children's stories. These services are also available at no charge to the physically handicapped—those unable to turn a printed page by themselves. If a blind person is offended by profanity or murder-mystery novels, he must specifically request that he not receive those types of materials from the state services.

One supplier of inspirational Christian materials for the blind is the Christian Record Braille Foundation (CRBF). Sponsored by the Seventh-day Adventist Church, the Christian Record, whose roots date back to 1899, is supported through gifts from the general public. All services, whether braille, large-print, or recorded magazines and books, full-vision books (which combine braille, ink print, and pictorial materials for blind parents to read to their sighted children), national camps for blind children, lending library, and more are offered free on a non-discriminatory basis. The foundation also sponsors the only personal visitation to the blind in North America, with over one hundred field workers who contact the blind in their homes and also serve as referral sources to assist the visually impaired in any way they can. CRBF is also concerned with the prevention of blindness. For this reason, free glaucoma screening clinics are sponsored by the foundation throughout the United States. Services offered from CRBF are on a nonsectarian basis. The foundation's address is 4444 South 52nd Street, Lincoln, Nebraska 68506.

There are some sixty other national organizations which supply services and materials to the blind. Three of the largest are the Library of Congress, National Service for the Blind and Physically Handicapped, 1291 Taylor Street, N.W., Washington, D.C. 20542; American Printing House for the Blind, 1839 Frankfort Avenue, Louisville, Kentucky 40206; and American Foundation for the Blind, 15 West

16th Street, New York, New York 10011. These organizations supply everything: watches, kitchen appliances, educational devices, braille writing equipment, and a score of other devices for the blind. Contact any of the above organizations and they will be more than happy to offer assistance.

The climactic book of the Bible describes vividly what the blind so long for. Revelation 1:7 says it so well: "Behold he cometh with clouds; and every eye shall see him. . . . " What a glorious calling ministers have to prepare those without sight to one day see Christ. As one blind man says, "I don't mind being physically blind; it's spiritual blindness that frightens me." Although we have no power to cure their physical blindness, we need to be more concerned with removing the spiritual blindness.

Quoting again from Miss Keller, whose life brought so much encouragement and joy to the blind of her era: "I can see, and that is why I can be so happy." Yes, blind persons long to "see," and they do want to be happy. God has commissioned each of us to help those less fortunate. It's our calling. It's up to each of us.

Lorraine Guild-Smith

10

Toward an Understanding of Parents with an Impaired Child

"You should start making plans to put him in an institution."

Glum silence followed, but rage overwhelmed me. How dare she make such a statement! I had gone to her in the hope that she would be more knowledgeable than the other M.D.'s. She had to be efficient. The fact that she would herself someday be a mother should have made her more capable in some way. Besides, my parents knew her parents from northern Alberta. Now that she was an M.D., educated in the United States and by chance in the same college town in Michigan, she just had to be someone with special abilities.

Yes, something wasn't quite right, but if the medical profession did not know what the problem was, they surely didn't have the right to make such a long-range prediction. After all, Kim was only two years old.

Kim was a beautiful baby boy with sturdy arms and legs, and a winning smile that would have made an ideal New Year's baby pinup. He was easy to keep happy and he slept well. There were no nights of walking the floor with Kim.

When Kim was nine months old, an appointment with a pediatrician was made to question the fact that he was not sitting up on his own or pushing to stand and take an interest in mobility. The young doctor found Kim to be sensitive to sound and responsive to movement that required eye coordination. Following this brief examination, I was told that Kim was just too heavy to hold up his own weight, but in time he would do so.

With this consolation, I buried myself in the task of my first year of teaching—a one-room school in northern British Columbia with grades one to eight. In my mid-twenties and with two years of college, which were obtained between two sets of baby bottles and being pregnant with Kim, my dream of teaching was again continued in earnest. Temporarily, the fears of Kim's development were dismissed.

After the school term was completed and the move to Michigan accomplished, the urgency of Kim's development was again foremost. Leads from the medical profession for determining the cause of his slowness were followed through with hope. This meant packing diapers and baby food, getting his two brothers, who were two and four years older, with their toys and food into the car, carrying Kim, who was extremely heavy, in and out of the vehicle, then waiting in small rooms with lines of people.

Whether a physical examination, EEG, or a blood test, these appointments were preceded by numerous tiring inquiries regarding family history and prenatal development. Questioning would dead end at:

"Was the pregnancy normal?"

"Yes."

"Did the baby look normal at birth?"

"Yes, except that he was more wrinkled than his brothers."

At two and a half years, Kim still did not walk. It was very painful to watch Kim's world seem to come to a standstill and see him left behind as others his age crawled, crept, walked, and said "mama." "Please, God, someone's got to care. Someone must have an answer as to why Kim doesn't walk. Please, God."

Shortly after settling down in Michigan, I became heavily involved in the leadership role of teaching children in church. There were many hours of creating, cutting, and pasting of objects that toddlers could hold while singing songs such as, "The flowers are gently swaying, swaying, swaying, showing God is love." But as the months progressed and Kim became visibly impaired, each soft, cuddly baby and toddler reminded me of what Kim could be, but wasn't. Kim could not sit in a chair without arms, he could not walk up to hold the flowers, he could not ask for offering to drop into the plate. One morning after an exceptionally creative presentation for the two- and three-year-olds, I walked away from the church duties without much explanation. Hopefully somebody understood.

Even the main church service deepened my sense of devastation, for there were monthly baby dedications where proud parents held their beautiful babies and they were blessed and dedicated to God. After several hasty exits from the church to wipe my overflowing eyes and control my sobbing body during these dedications, I found it much more tranquil to listen to the service over the radio station. I then could not see the happy parents with their "bundles of joy."

There was a three-hour trip to the prestigious University of Michigan's Children's Hospital. It was another gloomy day, both environmentally and mentally. Of course numerous forms needed to be filled out. This was followed by additional verbal inquiries. More bodies in white coats peered at and probed at Kim. Nothing. Just another costly visit.

Once back home, a question that was not answered during the interviewing at the Children's Hospital kept recurring. Has there been a PKU check? Whatever that was, it was suggested that Kim have one. Back to the local hospital lab for a blood test. A week later the results were reported to be negative.

Before the results of this blood test were returned, however, a home urine test was devised for PKU by Kim's uncle, then an undergraduate student and now a practicing D.O. A drop of ten percent ferric chloride was placed on Kim's wet diaper. Immediately a blue-green color appeared. It was positive! This meant that Kim had PKU. In a haze as to the meaning of all this, I notified the hospital at the University of Michigan. Kim was to be admitted immediately.

A flood of explanatory literature and verbal explanations followed. I learned that PKU is the abbreviated term for phenylketonuria, the result of an inborn defect in the body's chemical processes. Those with PKU are unable to properly metabolize phenylalanine, an amino acid found in some foods. Proteins are broken down into amino acids which are used as building blocks with the aid of enzymes. In PKU, a particular enzyme is lacking. As a result, the amino acid phenylalanine is not utilized by the body. Therefore, large amounts collect in the blood. If the phenylalanine is too high, the brain does not develop normally.

A stay at the hospital was necessary to assess the level of phenylalanine in the blood, then determine the amount that could be allowed in the diet. By following a prescribed diet, the phenylalanine content of the blood was to stay within the desired range. A month and a medical bill of approximately one thousand dollars later, Kim was home. His previous eating habits had to be disregarded as he needed to be kept on a special low-phenylalanine diet.

The practical application of this diet involved numerous details. The specific protein content of a varied assortment of fruits, fruit juices, vegetables, and some cereal products was reviewed. Various means of preparing foods with a low-phenylalanine supplement which substituted for meat, eggs, milk, and breads were studied. Accuracy in measuring was emphasized. Colors, flavors, textures, and finger food, all important learning experiences in the development of the young child, were considered within the limitation of the diet prescription. From sample menus, total daily protein intake needed calculation. Written records of the kind, amount, and phenylalanine content of foods eaten needed to be kept. All this was time-consuming and extremely bewildering.

Dairy milk, a basic food for most babies, was no longer allowed. In its place a product from Mead-Johnson Company called Lofenalac, which is low in phenylalanine content, was used. A blender or egg beater was necessary to mix the powder with water into a smooth formula for drinking. This milk smelled differently. It took concentrated effort on my part to avoid making a face during its preparation.

When the public health nurse brought two cans of Lofenalac, she also had recipes for cookies and other baked goods to be made with this substitute. As a whole egg contained 355 milligrams of phenylalanine (more than Kim's total daily allowance), cookies for Kim needed to be made without eggs, regular milk, or flour. Lofenalac substituted for all of these ingredients. The results of hours in the kitchen: cookies that dissipated into crumbs before Kim could get them into his mouth.

Mealtime became a fiasco. After Kim was placed in a chair at the table, his strategy was to silently take inventory of the carrots, green beans, and potato on his plate, then survey the contents of what his brothers had been served. Quick as a flash he would have his hand in someone's lasagna or other forbidden morsels he had once been allowed to enjoy.

The bottom line to the personal agony of implementing this treatment program and yet watching Kim regress is that dietary management for PKU must begin in the earliest weeks of a child's life to prevent interference with the normal development of the brain and central nervous system. PKU infants are normal at birth and during infancy.

When diagnosed, the adverse symptoms in phenylketonuria can be prevented or ameliorated with a low-phenylalanine diet. Once brain development has been retarded, the process can only be arrested but not reversed. It is the first month of life that is critical in preventing the irreversible consequences, but Kim was almost three years old before he was diagnosed!

As a PKU child, Kim's brain damage is in the area of motor development. It was learned that the frontal portion of the brain, which is in the developmental stage until approximately the age of three, deals with motor development. Motor activities are those associated not only with walking and running, but also with verbal output. It was the latter prognosis that I could not accept. How could it be possible that such a healthy and happy baby would never utter a word? With such a sturdy body and well-developed legs and arms, it was impossible to comprehend that Kim would also never walk!

Again, with desperate urgency, someone professional who might be able to help was sought. During the Christmas season when Kim was three and a half years old, a trip to the Institutes for the Achievement of Human Potential in Philadelphia was suddenly made when some other family could not keep their appointment.

More strange terminology and foreign concepts—pons, cortex, midbrain, hemispheric dominance, programming, opportune environment, augmentation of the sensory environment, and on. This was just the introduction to the major program of therapy called patterning which was to take Kim through the crawling and creeping stages so that he could eventually walk. Methods and procedures for this and instruction for additional sensory stimuli were provided in detail by the Institute.

Once back home, the first step was to locate volunteers who would assist with the patterning sessions exactly three hours apart, four times a day, every day of the week. For effective patterning, four people were needed to simultaneously coordinate the movement of Kim's legs, arms, and head while he lay prone on a covered table. There was a long box to build, eight inches high with a cord for a ceiling, in which Kim could learn how to crawl. There were also eleven daily sessions in which a plastic mask was placed over Kim's mouth and nose to force him to breathe back his own carbon dioxide.

The effort required to reorganize the household for Kim's new program loomed as an awesome responsibility. Especially intimidating was to approach strangers in the community and ask them to contribute several minutes a day or a week to assist with the patterning.

It was extremely distressing to ask for help, particularly knowing that this was on a continuing basis. My feelings were repressed, yet it was my expectation that somehow people would discover how much their support was needed. But when someone was asked to help, there was fear that I would be indebted to that person, and I just did not have the motivation, the energy, or the time to return a favor.

Disorganization permeated my being. My ability to concentrate and retain information was limited. Conversations with acquaintances would hold my attention for only a short period. Functioning at even the simplest level became a struggle.

An exhausting day did not end with a deep sleep. Many nights were restless. Far worse than tossing most of the night, however, were the mornings. There seemed to be a momentary period shortly after awakening when everything disappointing was forgotten. Then, like a tidal wave, the remembrance of Kim would engulf me. This quicksand of grief made it difficult to move into action.

* * * * *

This self-disclosure of the shattered dream of a young mother and now single parent will hopefully bring the reader a new perspective of some of the emotional and psychological stresses that are typical of the parents of an impaired child. In one chapter it is not possible to deal with the comprehensive treatment of parental adjustment, nor is this intended to be a full report of the research available on counseling techniques. It is, instead, written for the purpose of awakening an awareness of a mother's reactions to a child who is disabled and of some of the problems brought to the family. There are, of course, many patterns of emotional adjustment. While the details differ from family to family, many of the stresses briefly discussed in the following content are similar regardless of the type of impairment.

SOME NORMAL PARENTAL REACTIONS

Shock

Parents realize that something is not quite right with their child as they gradually come to that conclusion by their own observation or when a professional makes the diagnosis. Discovering the concrete fact that one has an impaired child is a heart-stopping, gut-level blow. The initial reaction is one of shock, disbelief, and numbness. The individual cannot believe that this is really happening. The nurse must have brought someone else's baby. They've heard of it happening to others but it could not happen to them. It is natural for parents to be emotionally unprepared for the arrival of a physically or mentally impaired child. Even the most adjusted parent encounters numerous crisis reactions.

Initial shock and its resultant feelings of disbelief will be related, at first, to the degree to which the disability is clearly visible or irreparable, states one counselor.

> A disability in a newborn child such as spastic paralysis or missing limbs is more inescapable, a constant visible reminder of one's pain. As such, it is initially less easy to deal with than the problem of a child who is born seemingly perfect but whose damage is internal, less visible. In the latter case, the stress and anxiety arise from the fact that the actual extent of the problem cannot be ascertained and the parents must be constantly at the mercy of the unpredictable future, watching, waiting, hoping (Buscaglia, 1975, p. 96).

Though most of the research done on initial reaction has been centered on the responses of the mother, it seems safe to generalize that the same reactions will involve the father, siblings, and other close family members. They are required to accept less than their ideal expectation of a perfect child.

During this period of shock, the parents tend not to perceive clearly. They may display docility, yet little, if any, of the information about the impairment is retained. A medical diagnosis, for most parents, is a mysterious label. They know little or nothing about such things as cerebral palsy, osteomyelitis, or spina bifida. But there is no escape. This stage of shock rapidly progresses into other reactions as the reality of the impairment prevails.

Anger

A doctor's explanation that a child is in some way impaired is met with silence and a sullen departure, characteristic of the behavior of people who are hurt. Though it may be unrecognized, some of this feeling overflows onto the professional person and a germ of hostility is implanted. Receiving unfavorable news can precipitate an attitude of resentment toward its unfortunate bearer. Medical personnel are frequently the focus of anger, for nonmedical people look up to them as being omniscient. (M.D., I too discovered, does not mean "Magnificent Deity.")

A hurt and frustrated parent may express anger at God and denounce Him. "If there is a God, why did He let our child be so helpless? Why does He make us suffer? There are a lot of really wicked people who don't have anything happen to them. If there is a God, why does He just pass over them?" For these parents, their handicapped child casts doubt on the existence of a just God.

Latent hostility lying dormant in distressed parents can show itself either in immediate or indirect means. It can be a verbal attack directed toward a person in a care-taking profession, or repressed anger may build up for a later explosion. This may be in the form of a tantrum, a destructive spree, or forbidden pleasures. Since adults find temper tantrums difficult to justify, they may turn to alcohol, drive at excessive speeds, or involve themselves in other types of behavior that increase their anger and compound their frustration.

Disappointment and Embarrassment

Parents regard their offspring as extensions of themselves. Their hope is that their child will become a reflection of their best selves. When this does not occur, they are ashamed. "How can I tell my friends and relatives? What will they think? They'll never forgive me for bringing a child that looks like this into the family."

Young parents, especially, feel pressured to make favorable impressions on their mates and their immediate family, as well as on all the uncles and aunts and cousins. A mother can feel that giving birth to an impaired child will discredit her and lessen the relatives' acceptance of her. A newborn with a cleft lip and palate may result in a mother not wanting to take the baby home until after corrective surgery. "I just don't want everyone to see her like this. What will they think of us with her face open like this?" The fear is that approval and much-needed support will be withdrawn by the family and acquaintances.

There is the question of baby announcements. Do parents send these out when their child has an impairment? Friends, relatives, and acquaintances are waiting to hear if it is a boy or girl. Where are the chocolates or cigars in celebration? A birth, for most families, is a time for congratulations, for gathering together and rejoicing. One couple, after much contemplation, sent out announcements with an added note stating that their doctor indicated that the newborn would have mental and physical problems.

Feeding, bathing, and dressing a baby are normally pleasurable activities for parents anticipating years of healthy development. However, these activities become burdensome when they continue into the school years and the prospects for improvement are dim. Many disappointments are temporary, but the thwarted expectations associated with having an impaired child are long-term and frequently intense. This disappointment can build resentment toward the child and toward friends and acquaintances who have physically normal children.

Parental embarrassment can be detected by their momentary loss of composure when they see someone looking at their impaired child. When asked about the handicap, they may not wish to discuss it and instead may steer the conversation to another topic. These natural reactions of embarrassment can give rise to anger and hostility toward anyone who directs attention toward their child. Unconscious of their submerged feelings, they may respond with hostility even to professional workers who need more information in their genuine efforts to help the family.

Relatives and friends, and, in fact, the general public, do not always readily accept a handicapped person. So where do impaired children or adults find friends? If a child is extremely limited in his activity, it is difficult to find acceptance. Parental hurt turns into anger when a visit to a friend's home leaves them unwelcome, or when other children refuse to include their impaired child in play activities.

Guilt

Since parents do not readily have scientific information available about the causes of impairment, they rationalize on the basis of their past experiences and information at hand. Parents may ascribe the impairment to a doctor's incompetence or negligence, or there may be suspicion that one's spouse is in some way responsible for the family having a handicapped child. It may be suspected that somewhere along the family line there is a "skeleton in the closet." Sometimes there is self-blame. Some mothers feel a personal responsibility for their child's impairment. A mother may attribute the condition to something she did or repeatedly thought about during the pregnancy. In self-incriminating reasoning she may be "sure" that a fall or related incident while carrying the baby caused the child to develop abnormally. Also, the mother may become the source of accusation to the point that not only relatives, but also her husband, treat her as if she were at fault.

Parents may conclude that having an impaired child is punishment for their sins. As children, these parents were probably taught to pray or wish for things very hard, and that as a reward, if they were very good, the prayer would be answered. Recalling some wrongdoings, a mother may state that God is making her pay for her sins by seeing to it that her daughter will not be able to do the things she did. Parents are often of the conviction that their own sins set the stage for their child's impairment.

Preoccupation with "who is to blame" can adversely color the parents' feelings about the child. Repeated disappointments and embarrassment, added to blame, are the genesis of less acceptance and affection for the impaired child. In the ups and downs of daily child care it is natural for feelings to fluctuate; annoyance coexists with feelings of love. However, when feelings of resentment toward a child become frequent, the parent may feel guilty about these emotions. The guilt over the occasional bitterness toward the helpless child can deeply affect the way in which the parents meet the demands of providing for the child's happiness and optimal development, as well as the living of their own lives.

Hope

To learn that one's child has a lifelong handicap and that he may never walk or talk like other children, go to a regular school, have friends, hold a job, get married, and do all the things that children grow up to do, leaves the parents with a strange mixture of anguish and helplessness. They are required to accept an unwelcomed reality. A natural defense against this is to doubt the diagnosis and prognosis, and seek more favorable opinions. As a result, parents may "shop"—taking their child to a number of professionals or clinics in hope that someone will assure them that nothing is seriously wrong or that through special help everything will be fine. Counsel based on a realistic evaluation of their child's condition may be rejected because the parents may be tuned to hear only what they want to be told. This truth rejection or denial can continue for many years. Though it may be an illusionary hope that some professional has the solution, as a veteran parent, the writer feels that this searching and hoping is an important phase in the mechanics of grieving the loss of a perfect child. A parent must feel that he or she has done everything possible, even though a great amount of the parent's time, energy, and money may be expended as a result.

When the reality of the impairment is established and accepted by the parents, they are free to move on to the task of working with the child. Belief in the possibility that change can occur motivates the parents to do everything they can to meet the habilitation needs of their child. They can now work with both hands and heart. Though continued nurturance may bring little change in the ability of the child, it is hope which sustains the parent beyond such disappointment and hurt. Both financial and physical resources may be depleted before the parents realize that everything they gave and did was not enough. But they did everything they could. There should then be little, if any, guilt of omission.

Powerlessness

July 20, 1969, was momentous, not particularly because the first American set foot on the moon, but because my son took his first unaided steps. After several months of continuous home therapy, Kim managed to bring himself up onto his feet from his usual kneeling position, balance himself steadily, and take his first walk. With a big, knowing smile on his face, he shuffled his way around the living room two and a half times. Kim was then four years and two months old.

Though Kim became capable of bringing himself up to stand and walk unaided, his most comfortable mode of movement was on his knees. He would hold himself erect while on his knees and propel himself on the carpeting or on the grass outdoors. When encouraged to stand, his posture was so stooped that he appeared to be in great pain in that position. Since Kim could not talk, there was no way for him to tell us.

Other aberrations of development became more pronounced. Kim's once smiling face and sparkling eyes began to show little variation in facial expression. An appearance of distance, remoteness, and aloneness became pronounced. Avoidance of eye-to-eye gaze left him in self-isolation and self-absorption. Kim no longer babbled like he did shortly after he was born. There was no evidence of inner language. He didn't even cry any more. The compulsion of obsessively repeating a simple activity developed. His favorites were turning light switches on and off endlessly, or spinning a plate on the floor, then flapping his hands to its rhythm. Rocking his body when sitting or lying down and hand-flapping became his main preoccupations.

In moments of overwhelming despair and helplessness, I'd wrap my arms around Kim while he was in a walking position on his knees (he was extremely big and heavy to lift), bury my face next to his beautiful, soft complexion, and sob. All the joy and brightness of living had evaporated from me. Devastating sorrow consumed me. This sorrow was hourly, daily, always present—an agonizing, shattering, distressing sorrow.

Parental helplessness and powerlessness go against the basic instincts of protecting, nurturing, and molding a delicate life. Because of the emphasis placed upon parenting by our society, adjusting to a child with a handicap magnifies the sense of inadequacy. Perhaps the most powerless-feeling parents are those whose children's impairments resulted from accident. An accident that suddenly leaves a child incapacitated seems so pointless and futile. To a man who successfully manipulates events to meet his wishes at work, but who is unable to control happenings surrounding the life of his child, this reality is extremely painful. Also there is the mother, usually the parent at home, who hourly wages the battle by herself, fiercely trying to bring about improvement in the child. The multitude of feelings are components of the sense of helplessness, an all-encompassing powerlessness.

Depression

Occasionally there are parents who do not seem to care and who make little effort to become involved in their child's problem. When asked about their understanding of the child's impairment, their reply reveals only a vague comprehension of the nature of the problem or any plan of treatment proposed by professionals. One clinician (McDonald, 1962, p. 168) states that " . . . even today there are children who get to clinics only because of the intercession of a minister, social worker, relative, or other interested person. It would appear that their parents could hardly care less about them." Perhaps in a few rare cases the parents do not care about the welfare of their child. However, from my viewpoint as a parent of an impaired child looking retrospectively on the past fourteen years, the most likely explanation for the lack of parental involvement is much more complicated.

First, the fruition of gnawing fear that a child is impaired sends the parent into numbness and shock. An aura of disbelief envelops the parent. Questions are asked, professionals try to answer, but technical replies about child care and volatile emotions heighten the confusion. The child's impairment does not improve on its own; rather, it becomes more pronounced as the months go by. Facing the necessity of multiple adjustments to a new mode of living in order to care for the child, when in a state of despair, is so difficult that healthful responses may be put off indefinitely. At times it is impossible to move into effective action. This emotional pain becomes so pervasive that the parent is overcome by a type of psychological unconsciousness more commonly referred to as depression.

One characteristic of depression is that of seeming apathy in which one does not want to act, think, or feel. From morning till late evening, the mother, in robot-like automation, performs the numerous home routines, plus the extra duties in the basic care for the special child. Father, likewise, goes to work in a dream-like trance. They are aware that they must resolve their feelings and face their challenges, but the emotional pain has anesthetized them.

It is not unusual for a woman to become depressed after the birth of her baby even if it is normal. This is termed "postpartum depression." Mothers who repress their mixed feelings about having the baby frequently become depressed. Having a baby and mothering it for many years is an enormous responsibility, particularly when the child is impaired and will constantly require an abnormal amount of care even into adulthood.

Parents of impaired children are prime candidates for the devastation of depression. In recent preparation for a seminar on the topic of depression and widowhood, this author found that the causes of America's number one health problem are nearly all experiences that parents of impaired children could encounter. Very briefly, some of the causes of depression as they could relate to such parents are: (1) excessive stress, (2) emotional conflicts, (3) low self-concept, (4) fatigue, and (5) physiological changes.

First, a large percentage of depressions are precipitated by stress (Minirth and Meier, p. 98). One of the most common stresses that incites depression is that of a loss, as in the loss of not having a perfectly functioning baby. Stress is also brought about by the adjustment to change. For parents of an impaired child, this change is not just a temporary one, but rather one of significant consequences in lifestyle. Second, emotional overloads and conflicts for lengthy periods result in depression. Anger is a common characteristic of depression. According to two psychiatrists, Minirth and Meier, depressions are loaded with angry feelings and unless the feelings are relieved, it is impossible to overcome the depression. These psychiatrists also state that guilt is another common cause of depression as it is a form of pent-up anger: anger toward oneself. Thirdly, a blow to the self-image is often a precipitating event that can lead to depression. Self-worth can be easily lowered when a mother finds she did not give birth to a perfect baby. As the parent becomes overextended physically and emotionally, fatigue permeates the being. This fourth cause of depression is the body's way of demanding isolation for the purpose of retrenchment.

In addition to these changes, the actual physiological changes should not be overlooked. Biochemical changes involving the brain amines take place in the nervous system during depression (Minirth and

Meier, p. 110). The segment of the brain known as the limbic is responsible for one's moods as it controls whether one feels elated, depressed, or even-tempered. Brain amines are neurotransmitters that float in the synapse between nerve cells. Depletion of these neurotransmitters is considered to be a factor in depression. Minirth and Meier state that pent-up anger causes depletion of these amines. Dysfunction of amines results in, among other things, insomnia, fatigue, appetite change, or heart palpitations.

Grief

These numerous feelings under discussion are natural reactions when parents learn that something is different with their child. The parents are grieving the lost dream of having a perfect baby. Mourning is an indication of concern and love. It is a gesture of caring. When a child is left with a physical or mental deficit, the caring parent has lost a portion of his or her complete future. To daily see a part of one's self being in need of endless care or unjustly struggling to meet basic needs leaves the parent devastated. This dilemma is unresolvable for the parents as they are unable to flawlessly do what parents instinctively seek to do.

A mother whose child had several impairments confided to the author that after her baby was diagnosed her emotional pain was so intense that she thought she "was going crazy." It wasn't until she had participated in counseling sessions and done much reading that she realized her responses were typical grief reactions. She stated that she experienced the classic grief reactions with all their ramifications as described by Kübler-Ross. Elisabeth Kübler-Ross (1969, p. 38) concluded through her research that there are five stages in the grieving process: (1) denial and isolation, (2) anger, (3) bargaining, (4) depression, and (5) acceptance.

Another researcher (Kavanaugh, 1972, p. 107) has listed seven stages to grieving: (1) shock, (2) disorganization, (3) volatile emotions, (4) guilt, (5) loss, (6) loneliness, and (7) relief and reestablishment. Other professionals categorize these in different units and with different terms. Nevertheless, the cataloguing of the stages in the grieving process does not imply that the stages are distinct or separate. These emotional states intertwine and overlap. They may be successive in the order listed or they may be in any other order. Certain stages may be passed by quickly, while others may linger for long periods. Flashbacks of the charged feelings may occur occasionally or repeatedly. Grief springs from the total experience of one's life as it takes on varied dimensions, with each parent responding differently. "Grief is a complex emotion. It is always personal. It is an extension of the inner life of a grieving individual. It reflects his values and his inner strength and weakness," states Edgar Jackson in *The Many Faces of Grief* (1977, p. 11).

LIFELINES FOR PARENTS

Some people live their entire life span without knowing real despair—the kind of inescapable despair that cannot be changed. Yet others must learn to live with such hopelessness. The only possible changes in such situations are in the person's feelings, attitudes, and lifestyle. He or she craves and definitely needs support to make the difficult adjustment. If Kim had died, there would have been an obituary so that the relatives and acquaintances would know I was grieving. Someone would probably have been sympathetic and would have tried to say something nice. Instead, friends and relatives just silently stared at Kim, then turned away. Kim was alive but experiencing a living death—a long-term assignment which would probably last my entire lifetime.

How did my church pastor help? This would be an ideal occasion to provide a glowing account of an experience which could furnish a precedent for future emulation. Perhaps if the setting had been in a small church, pastoral involvement would have been apparent. Being one member among approximately two thousand did not lend itself to much individualized recognition. Based upon a first telephone call from the head pastor several years later when I was "head of the household," it was best that pastoral involvement was limited. The phone call was most untimely (just before the first morning service as I was preparing to leave), and most disturbing. His inquisitions were prodding and somewhat judgmental. The first church activity was half over by the time the conversation ended, and by then I was too upset to leave for the main service. In fact, I don't recall leaving the apartment for the entire day. This was my experience; hopefully others have more positive interactions. This is not saying that pastoral interaction should be avoided. There are, I'm sure, many tactful, empathetic "men of God" who know how to perform their duties skillfully.

When a parent is adjusting to a cruelly painful reality, he has only two choices. He can (1) face his feelings and problems, accept them, and try to resolve them, or (2) he can pretend they do not exist and try pushing them out of his existence. If the latter is chosen, these repressed feelings unconsciously create psychological patterns of defense to keep the emotions in check. Defense patterns, whether they are excuses, blaming others, scapegoating, sublimating, or over-compensating, are formed under great stress. They are not a permanent solution. Denied feelings accumulated under the disguise of self-control tend to escape through the safety valve of numerous symptoms: headaches, intestinal upsets, shallow sleep, depression, and disorganization. "Keeping emotions in check takes great energy. Playing an unreal role is not easy. Feigning well-being is often transparent and hollow. In most cases, at some time or other, the parent will be forced to face his true feelings regarding himself, his family, the child who is disabled, and the disability" (Buscaglia, 1975, p. 100).

Genuine help must be of the type that provides the opportunity for exploring and bringing to the surface all the unhappy feelings that have not been faced. It is not the duty of a counselor (not even a professedly Christian one) to judge such feelings as wrong or shameful. Statements such as, "You shouldn't feel that way," or, "It's un-Christian to say that," are not part of therapy. Condescending comments or hasty mannerisms are of no consolation. They serve only to increase the hostility and deepen the withdrawal of the anxiety-ridden parent. The process of facing up to one's emotions, especially strong feelings, is painful. It requires insight, strength, intelligence, and honesty.

> . . . when we experience deep pain of an emotional nature, we need to be approached with great sensitivity; we need to be accepted in an upset state; we need to feel we can trust others enough to let down our guard, say what we choose and not be judged or criticized. In fact, the fewer the words, the better; the caring communicates itself without words if it is genuine (Buscaglia, 1975, p. 153).

An eclectic type of counseling approach is outlined by Clinebell in *The Mental Health Ministry of the Local Church*. Effective pastoral counseling ingredients, according to Clinebell (1972, p. 218), consist of: (a) establishing a growing therapeutic relationship through warm, non-judgmental concern; (b) disciplined listening to and reflecting of feelings (this encourages the catharsis of bottled-up feelings which is like draining the infection from a wound); (c) seeking an understanding of the person's "internal frame of reference"; (d) gaining a diagnostic impression concerning the nature of his concerns, weaknesses, and inner resources; and (e) directing an approach to help based on the tentative diagnosis.

The eclectic method adapts itself to the demands of the situation and allows the counselor freedom to use either a directive or a nondirective approach, or a blend of the two. This method is flexible rather than diagnostic. The aim is to aid the person in helping himself. If he is emotionally charged, he is encouraged through a supportive atmosphere to unleash his feelings. When he is in need of information and advice, he is provided with such.

Some pastoral counselors may feel that their position within a church necessitates a more directive and authoritarian approach. The pastor, in his authoritarian role, may choose the goals and then advise the parent to move toward them. Provided there is no underlying psychological condition which the pastor-counselor does not understand, provided the pastor-counselor judges correctly, and provided the person is willing to take direction from the counseling pastor, little harm is likely to be done to the growth potential of the parent and the possible habilitation of the impaired child. Instead of a dogmatic technique which manipulates and controls, it would be appropriate to explore together alternative ways of establishing or reestablishing patterns of conduct. A healthy outcome is dependent upon the freedom of the person to express himself, determine his goal, and eventually solve his own problem.

Buscaglia, in *The Disabled and Their Parents* (1975, p. 279), states that

> Counselors cannot tell the family what to feel or do; they must allow them to find their own insights, charter their own paths, and encourage them and involve them in ego-satisfying and building experiences. The family members need praise, alternatives to behavior, and, at times, strong arms to lean on or a broad shoulder on which to cry. They will need to know that the counselor cares, that they are unique individuals of worth working together cooperatively, and that they are capable of working through their own problems to satisfying conclusions.

The multitude of complications presented when a parent has an impaired child lends itself to a variety of needs, situations, and techniques. As a result, counseling situations will vary. The pastor can be needed for: (a) marriage and family counseling, (b) supportive (including crisis) counseling, (c) counseling for referral, (d) short-term educative and decision-making counseling, (e) superego counseling, (f) informal counseling, (g) group counseling, and (h) religious-existential problem counseling (Clinebell, 1972, p. 218). Several of these types can be utilized in the same counseling situation.

Parents with unsolved problems may be immobilized by guilt, anger, fear, and pain. As a result, counseling needs to deal with both self-discovery and information giving. During these interactions, the counselor should keep in mind specific goals (Buscaglia, 1975, pp. 278, 279):

> To help the parents to see that the special child is a child first and a child with a disability second.

> To understand the issues and facts involved in the disabling condition so as to best be able to help the child in a constructive manner.

> To assist the parents and child to understand their unique feelings which have been aroused by the advent of a disability.

> To aid the parents and child to accept the disability emotionally and intellectually without devaluing the individual possessing it.

> To help the child and parents in continuing to develop their unique potentials together, and independently, toward their own self-actualization.

In any single situation, the counselor may find himself asking very specific questions, listening intently, acting as arbitrator and resource person, and even giving direct information. Due to the uniqueness of the counseling situation, three family-related topics are discussed and some community resources are explored to aid the pastor-counselor in his role of guiding the parents of an impaired child.

Sensitivity to Terminology

"Mom, what does 'retarded' mean? Jimmy said that Kim was retarded. What did he mean?" inquired Delroy, Kim's oldest brother, as he rushed in from being with the neighbor children. This sincere and candid question from a seven-year-old caught me off guard. It was the first time that I heard the term "retarded" applied to Kim. Suddenly I had difficulty coming to grips with a word which I had at one time used with ease. What bothered me, too, was that the youthful speaker had not only conveyed his biased ideas and feelings by its usage, but he was also shaping the concepts and attitudes of the little listeners. I feared what was in store for Kim and his brothers: ridicule, embarrassment, pain.

Certain terminology is considered to be offensive and in poor taste. Even Ann Landers has been asked to address the issue of the power of words in her column. Her crusade is to help educate the public to use the correct and more contemporary terms: "Down's Syndrome" rather than the negative and old-fashioned term "mongol" or "mongoloid"; "seizures" instead of "epileptic fits"; "deaf and mute" instead of "deaf and dumb"; and "Hansen's disease" instead of "leprosy." In addition, "learning disabled" or "developmentally disabled" are more acceptable than "mentally retarded".

On more subtle semantic issues, Beatrice Wright, in *Physical Disability—A Psychological Approach*, argues that everyone should be tactful with terminology, especially when relating to the disabled. She explains that we should refer to "a person who is physically disabled" rather than "a physically disabled person," for the former phrase considers that individual as a person first, with the disability secondary. She also rejects the word "handicapped" on the premise that the term deals more with the accumulated obstacles, as there are not only physical but also societal and interpersonal limitations with which this person must cope. A disability is a type of medical condition, but it may also become a handicap when a disability is allowed to debase or debilitate one emotionally or intellectually, to prevent one from achieving a desired goal, or to preclude one's ability to fare for himself.

Cultural and societal stigmatization of those who are different is aptly described by Pearl Buck in her book *The Child Who Never Grew*. While living in China, her severely mentally and physically impaired daughter was not recognized as different, for at that time the Chinese cared for them as they would any other child. In that culture the disabled were accepted as a fact of life. It was not until Mrs. Buck and her daughter arrived in the Western culture that they encountered prejudice. Then Mrs. Buck began to perceive her daughter as being abnormal and then she, too, began to respond and treat her differently.

An Impaired Child Needs Two Caring Parents

That children have two parents when they start life is a biological fact. Mothers of impaired children, however, frequently find themselves in a one-parent role in which they are nurse, physical therapist, purchasing agent, cook, cleaning lady, chauffeur, and fill-in for all types of emergencies. In this type of situation a wife feels that she doesn't have a husband, for he never helps with the feeding, bathroom duties, putting on of braces, therapy, and other responsibilities with the impaired child. On the other hand, the husband may complain that his wife doesn't want to go anyplace with him and that she is too tired or too tense to be affectionate. The father may escape his share of responsibility by working long hours or finding other activities away from home. The problem can have many other variations, especially when in-laws and other relatives interfere. Having a child with a handicap puts severe pressure on the bonds of matrimony.

With the best intentions, someone may think, "At least they have each other for comfort." Certainly a husband and wife having each other for comfort would be a logical solution. However, too much can be expected of a mate and too little received. It is thought that grieving spouses can lean on each other. "But you cannot lean on something bent double from its own burden," states Harriet Schiff in *The Bereaved Parent*. "Just when our expectations assure us we would have all sorts of support from a mate, we discover he is just about the last person who can really help. Society has conditioned us to believe we now would be one grieving pair. Instead we have two bereaved people." Each parent mourns as an individual. Each bears his or her pain. A mate cannot bear sorrow for another. A wife should not expect her husband to be a tower of strength when he is feeling the same pain she is. Likewise, a husband should recognize that his wife would listen to him if his feelings did not tend to pull her into a low. Added to the complication, the spouses will find that they are not at the same stage of emotional state, or that they are not experiencing the feelings simultaneously.

The sameness of each day, particularly if it brings no new hope in the developmental pattern of a child, gnaws at the inner being. Adjustments need to be made in expectations, budgets, and dreams for the future. This enormous mental calisthenic tends to make the parents view one another, the other children, and the entire world through an anguished perception. This state of continuous despair should not continue, for the sake of every family member's mental health. It is critical to alleviate this pain as gently and quickly as possible. Buscaglia (1975, p. 147) encourages the parents to

> Take care of your child with his very special needs, reach out for help and direction, but take care of yourself, too. Stay alert to the needs of your husband (wife) and other youngsters in the family. More than anything else, your exceptional child will benefit from intactness within his family group.

A parent who has an impaired child is always a person first. He or she is a parent, of course, but this individual is more than just a parent. This parent also has other roles—husband or wife, son or daughter, worker, consumer, taxpayer, and so many others. The birth of a child with a handicap should not take from the parents their rights as people. They still have the right to time alone, for each other, for recreation, for friends, and for other activities that are important to them.

> To raise an exceptional child in our culture will demand the best parents have to give. In fact, it will perhaps become their life's second greatest challenge. The main challenge to any person will always be his own growth, development, and self-actualization. One can only give to his child, or anyone else, what he himself has and knows. This may sound selfish but it becomes less so when one considers that ignorance only creates more ignorance, while only wisdom can create wisdom. No dead person has ever taught life, as no loveless person has ever been able to teach love. One must have these qualities first, before sharing them with others (Buscaglia, 1975, p. 90).

The Welfare of Other Siblings is at Stake

The reality of the possible needs of my other sons was brought into jarring focus during a brief parent-teacher conference when the middle son's kindergarten teacher informed me that "Kirby needs more attention at home." Dismayed, then annoyed by such abrupt advice, I failed to inquire about my son's actions that precipitated this diagnosis by his teacher. Personally, I had not perceived this need, but then I was preoccupied with my own emotional disequilibrium.

In parental zeal to create a comfortable world for the child with a handicap, the husband and wife not only neglect each other but also overlook the needs of the rest of the siblings to be listened to, to be loved, and to be disciplined fairly. Signs of sibling stress are often more difficult to detect at home than at school, for the family unit is so much a part of the daily home scene that subtle signs for help may not be readily observed. Attention-getting actions, chronic fatigue, stomachaches, and poor schoolwork are some of the possible results of anxieties that the siblings of impaired children can manifest (White, 1978, p. 109).

> The children in the family suffer the same tensions, humiliations, stares, comments, taunts, rejections, frustrations, emotional fatigue, and other assorted aggravations that parents undergo, to a more exquisite degree. They don't have the parental reinforcement of the handicapped child being their own flesh and blood (Stigen, 1975, p. 63).

A great amount of attention in a variety of time-consuming efforts is bestowed upon a child with a handicap. Often the brothers and sisters "get stuck" with the care of their slower family member. They hear praise for something that everybody took for granted when they accomplished the same thing. "Big deal, she put on her shoes by herself. She should; she's seven!" When outdoors, they may witness a neighborhood child spit on their brain-damaged sister, the spittle trailing down the pink cheek of this gentle, puzzled child who came out to merely watch the others play. Being the sibling of an impaired child is a tough job.

SOME LOCAL COMMUNITY RESOURCES

Parent-to-Parent

"Professional advice was okay, but I needed to talk with a mother who had a child like mine—someone who really knew how I felt," a mother told me. Parents have a right to interact with other families who have children with disabilities. They need such friendship and support, not to create a common bond in disability but to assure them that they are not alone with such problems. In sharing, they have the opportunity to learn of new ideas and helpful procedures for being more effective parents. These parents will also be able to share an emotional understanding and growth. It is most difficult for parents to accept the handicapping conditions of their children. Through the leadership of a professional and the support of other parents, they can break through the period of denial of the handicap to plan for the child's future. Perhaps they can eventually become involved in the development of community groups which can bring about changes in laws, and in creating educational and job opportunities for their exceptional children.

Intermediate School District

The Intermediate School District acts as an intermediary between the State Department of Education and the local school districts. Among its responsibilities is the development of a plan to implement special education programs and services throughout the county. It employs many ancillary personnel such as school psychologists, occupational therapists, physical therapists, teacher consultants, and teachers of the homebound/hospitalized, all of whom work with local school districts in the operation of special education programs.

Educational Services

According to the U.S. Department of Health, Education, and

Welfare, the 1978 statistics indicate that approximately twelve percent of school-aged children are handicapped. Numerically, this totals about 5.5 million children. When including the pre-schoolers and the 18-21 age range, the estimate is 7 to 8 million handicapped children (U.S. DHEW, 1979, p. 1). In November 1975, Congress passed the Education for All Handicapped Children Act (Public Law 94-142), thereby mandating that by September 1, 1978, all school-aged handicapped children in the United States be assured "a free appropriate public education." This Act specifies a number of activities that schools must engage in to ensure that handicapped children receive the rights they have been guaranteed. These implementing regulations extend not only to state educational agencies and local school systems, but also to state correctional facilities and other state agencies such as welfare departments and departments of mental health.

Who are classified as handicapped eligible to receive services? "Handicapped children, as defined by PL 94-142 regulations, are those who are evaluated in accordance with procedures specified in the regulations and who, as a result, are found to be mentally retarded, hard-of-hearing, deaf, speech impaired, visually handicapped, seriously emotionally handicapped, orthopedically impaired, deaf-blind, multi-handicapped, learning disabled, or otherwise health-impaired children that would need special education or related services" (U.S. DHEW, 1979, p. 7). For eligibility, the degree of handicap can vary from mild to severe.

Funding aid is available to any state that makes a "free appropriate education" accessible to all children. By mid-1979, all states except New Mexico had applied for funds under PL 94-142. Provision of special education and related services for the variety of handicapping conditions is broad. To assist in assessing the status of an educational program at a particular school, it is necessary to understand four major components in PL 94-142: (1) identification, (2) education in the "least restrictive environment," (3) individual planning, and (4) due process rights (Daly, 1979, p. 40).

Identification: The schools are required to seek out handicapped children and have specialists test and evaluate, without charge, the special educational needs of impaired children. One test (such as a written IQ test) or a single procedure is not sufficient. The testing devices must also be free of cultural or other bias. Should the school not have adequate testing, parents may get an independent evaluation for which the school can cover the expenses, provided the need for testing is demonstrated by a special hearing procedure (see *Due Process Rights*).

Education in the "Least Restrictive Environment": A handicapped child is to be placed in the "least restrictive environment that suits his or her special needs," meaning a program as close as possible to that of a non-handicapped child. An impaired child is to be removed from the regular educational environment only when the nature or severity of the handicap is such that education in regular classes with the utilization of supplementary aids and services cannot be achieved satisfactorily. For some children, the least restrictive environment means a full schedule in the regular classroom with perhaps a couple of hours of special instruction per week. For other youngsters, this means learning in a self-contained classroom with those of similar problems, then joining some activities like music and art education with pupils from the regular classes. Some severely impaired children might receive their full-time program in a self-contained classroom, or at a special institution such as a school for the hearing impaired. Where it is considered to be in the interests of the child, instruction in the home can be covered. All of these services are at public expense.

Public Law 94-142 emphasizes the integration of impaired children not only into academic classes, but also into nonacademic courses and extracurricular activities such as art, music, industrial arts, home economics, special interest clubs sponsored by the schools, athletics, lunch periods, and counseling services. These experiences are of special importance for those whose educational needs may require them to be solely with other impaired children during most of the academic day.

Individual Planning: Each child identified as handicapped must have a detailed "individualized educational program" (IEP) written for him. The school is to notify parents of the evaluation findings and include parents in the process of decision-making regarding how and in what circumstances their child will be educated. A child's IEP must be reviewed at least once a year. IEP formats can vary, but they must state the child's current capabilities, list specific goals for the school year, and detail the extent of services that will be provided.

Though individualized plans for pupils are utilized by many teachers, the IEP is unique because of the requirement that parents participate. Parents are encouraged to be involved in the development of the program and they must agree to the contents. They can also challenge the program if they wish. However, an IEP is not a contract. A teacher cannot be held legally responsible for a child who does not progress according to schedule.

Due Process Rights: PL 94-142 outlines appeal and hearing procedures available for parents who don't agree with the diagnosis for their child, with the IEP, or with its implementation. Procedures vary from state to state, but the usual sequence is an informal hearing first; next, a formal hearing at the district level; finally, a formal hearing at the state level. When failing to get satisfaction at these hearings, parents may appeal to the appropriate state court.

Financial Assistance: Two Possible Sources

A developmentally disabled child or adult may be eligible to receive monetary assistance through a program called Supplemental Security Income. SSI provides a monthly stipend to those with little or no income (low income, high medical bills, few assets such as savings accounts). If the child is developmentally disabled, the parent can apply for SSI for him or her. If the child is over eighteen, or under eighteen but married, he or she may be able to get SSI as an adult.

The local Social Security office can provide information on eligibility. To locate the office, check the telephone directory under "Social Security Administration" or "U.S. Government—Social Security Administration." The following information will be needed: birth certificate, paycheck stubs, rent receipts, and bankbooks. If the child is under eighteen, the parents' income will be checked.

Once the Social Security office has determined that the child is eligible for SSI based on the parents' income, they will need proof that he or she is impaired enough to get SSI. Written proof will be needed from a medical doctor, psychologist, neurologist, or other person who has professionally dealt with the child. After the Social Security office has the information needed about the child's disability, the information will be sent to its medical agency for it to determine eligibility for SSI. This may take several weeks for approval.

The Department of Public Health, in addition to diagnostic and medical services, may also provide ongoing medical service at no cost for children whose parents or guardians are experiencing financial difficulty due to low income and extended medical expenses. The criteria for receiving financial assistance from the Department of Public Health tend to be flexible. A family need not be at the poverty level or receiving welfare services to qualify for assistance. Parents may be requested to reimburse the state for costs incurred for some types of medical service at some future date. The amount and method of reimbursement is dependent upon family income, assets, and needs.

Sheltered Employment and Pre-employment Training

Besides pre-employment training, there may be available centers for employment of adults with impairments. Vocational rehabilitation centers provide adult work activity, work evaluations, and work adjustment training. Transportation is usually provided to and from these centers. The Department of Vocational Rehabilitation also provides job training, counseling, testing, and job placement for persons who are handicapped.

Recreation and Informal Education

The Mental Health Department, the YWCA, and the Association for Exceptional Children and Adults, each or collectively, sponsor social club-like activities: field trips, dances, games. A home living consultant from the Mental Health Department may be available as a homebound service to adults who have the potential for improving their daily living skills. This service is provided in small groups with emphasis on activities such as exercising, cooking, shopping, and budgeting.

Foster Care

Foster care homes, under the direction of the Department of Social Services, provide a supportive twenty-four-hour residential environment. This program is designed for those who, because of infirmity, physical or emotional handicap, mental retardation, or age, require a protected home situation and some personal supervision to remain in the community. In this home-like setting, many individuals find their needs met much better than is possible in a large institution or hospital.

Institutions or State Homes

All pre-admissions are processed through the local community mental health department for placement of a developmentally disabled person in a state home. The request is usually made by the parent or by a professional such as a medical doctor, teacher, psychologist. The mental health department does not seek out families with developmentally disabled children; therefore it is important that a referral be made to them. Once a referral has been made, a life consultant worker, also known as a social worker, is assigned. The life consultant then makes contact with the family and begins to gather the necessary information for the forms. Birth, medical, family, educational, and psychological records are requested. To parents, the answering of numerous questions and filling out of forms may seem endless. However, to the life consultant this information is essential as the efforts must be well documented or the referral will not be accepted. The parents need to go through "the grind," for this same type of cross examination will face the life consultant as she or he works with the state agencies. During this application process, the life consultant, with the parents, investigates all alternatives to institutionalization. The usual alternatives are nursing homes (if the child is severely impaired) or foster homes.

Once documentation is completed, a pre-admission conference date is set with the staff of the state home. The prepared document is reviewed by the staff with the parents to assess the developmental needs of the child, to check the community resources available to meet these needs, and to assess the appropriateness of seeking placement in the institution. Admission date is set a few days after the pre-admission conference at the convenience of the parents. The child is placed on a thirty-day trial basis, during which time further evaluation is done to determine whether his training and educational needs are met by institutional placement. The child is then officially admitted or discharged.

BIBILIOGRAPHY

Buck, Pearl. *The Child Who Never Grew.* New York: John Day Company, 1950.

Buscaglia, Leo. *The Disabled and Their Parents: A Counseling Challenge.* Thorofare, N.J.: Charles B. Slack, Inc., 1975.

Clinebell, Howard J., Jr. *The Mental Health Ministry of the Local Church.* Nashville, Tenn.: Abingdon Press, 1972.

Daly, Margaret. "Handicapped Children in the Classroom—What 'Mainstreaming' Is All About." *Better Homes and Gardens*, September 1979, pp. 38-49.

Dempsey, John J. *Community Services for Retarded Children.* Baltimore: University Park Press, 1975.

Heisler, Verda. *A Handicapped Child in the Family: A Guide for Parents.* New York: Grune and Stratton, 1972.

Jackson, Edgar N. *The Many Faces of Grief.* Nashville, Tenn.: Abingdon Press, 1977.

Katz, Alfred H. *Parents of the Handicapped.* Springfield, Ill.: Charles C. Thomas, 1961.

Kavanaugh, Robert E. *Facing Death*. New York: Penguin Books, Inc., 1972.

Kübler-Ross, Elisabeth. *On Death and Dying*. New York: Macmillan, 1969.

McDonald, Eugene T. *Understand Those Feelings*. Pittsburgh: Stanwix House, Inc., 1963.

Mead Johnson Laboratories. *Phenylketonuria: Low Phenylalanine Dietary Management with Lofenalac*. Evansville, Ind., 1965.

Minirth, Frank B., and Meier, Paul D. *Happiness Is a Choice: A Manual in the Symptoms, Causes, and Cures of Depression*. Grand Rapids, Mich.: Baker Book House, 1978.

Parkes, Colin Murry. *Bereavement: Studies of Grief in Adult Life*. New York: International Universities Press, Inc., 1972.

Paterson, George W. "Ministering to the Family of the Handicapped Child." *Journal of Religion and Health* 14 (1975):165-176.

Schiff-Sarnoff, Harriet. *The Bereaved Parent*. New York: Penguin Books, 1977.

Stigen, Gail. *Heartaches and Handicaps: An Irreverent Survival Manual for Parents*. Palo Alto, Calif.: Science and Behavior Books, Inc., 1976.

U.S. Department of Health, Education, and Welfare. *Phenylketonuria*. Washington, D.C.: Government Printing Office, 1965.

U.S. Department of Health, Education, and Welfare, Office of Education. *Progress Towards a Full Appropriate Public Education: A Report to Congress on the Implementation of Public Law 94-142: The Education of All Handicapped Children Act*. January 1979.

Webster, Elizabeth J. *Professional Approaches With Parents of Handicapped Children*. Springfield, Ill.: Charles C. Thomas, 1976.

White, Robin. *The Special Child*. Boston: Little, Brown, 1978.

Roy E. Hartbauer

11

Counseling Persons with Communicative Disorders

Divinity students often take courses in Voice and Diction for Ministers. During these courses they not only study the proper production and use of the speech mechanism, but they are told how to lessen the possibilities of acquiring any of the speech disorders themselves.

Speech-language is considered abnormal when it interferes with communication, calls attention to itself, or causes its possessor to be maladjusted. The untrained pastor may be aware that a parishioner's speech is not right but may not know how to discuss the "impediment in the speech" of the person under consideration.

To assist the pastor in his observations and understanding of the problem, he should know that there are two broad categories of speech-language disorders: organic, in which there is an anatomical or physiological deviation from normal, and functional, in which all structures are normal and are capable of normal functioning but are being used incorrectly.

Regardless of the type of suspected speech, language, or hearing disorder, the pastor should refer the person to a speech-language pathologist or audiologist. Speech-language pathologists and audiologists do not work under the supervision of a medical doctor. They are independent professionals with their own organization and certifying boards. They cross-reference patients with the medical profession when it is proper to do so. The writer, for example, will not work with a voice disorder without a physician's clearance that there is no medically related pathology. The physician, on the other hand, refers his voice disorder cases to speech pathologists for rehabilitative procedures. Medical doctors do not have the training to satisfactorily do diagnostic speech, language, and hearing workups.

VOICE DISORDERS

The most common speech disorder among ministers, *per se*, is a problem with the voice caused by misuse. About ten years ago a pastor whose voice was almost inaudible came to the writer's office upon referral from an otolaryngologist (ear, nose, and throat doctor). He had been told by the doctor that he had vocal nodules, which are growths on the vocal cords. The man was particularly anxious about it because he was to begin a six-week (five nights a week) public evangelistic campaign in three days and wanted his throat problem resolved by then. He was told that the problem could not be resolved that quickly and that what he really needed in order to save his voice and ultimately his career was a month of total vocal rest. After that, his speaking habits needed to be retrained with elimination of the old, damaging habits. He had a legitimate concern for his evangelistic program, because all arrangements and all advertising had been done and it would be tragic to call it off at so late a date. The problem was resolved by a telephone conversation with the pastor's conference president. Another evangelist from the conference office was called in to be the speaker. There was better-than-expected rehabilitation of the afflicted voice and about three and a half weeks later the minister was participating in the evangelism *and* his career was salvaged. He is doing public evangelism today.

There are three broad categories of voice disorders: loudness, pitch, and quality. We will continue to refer to the voice disorders of ministers to help emphasize their relevance to the clergy. Ministers can have the same vocal problems as cheerleaders, side-show barkers, and anyone else who makes extensive, yet incorrect use of the voice. Observation of preachers on television and radio as well as in the churches subjects the observer to hollerers, screamers, and other persons who speak very loudly. It may be their personal style or the style expected by the people of their denomination. If they are using such loudness without proper training, there is a probability that they will become handicapped by virtue of voice problems. You, as a fellow minister, may find it easier to relate to their problems than to the same problems in laymen.

The symptoms of any voice disorder are hoarseness or harshness, stridency, pain in the throat, fatigue of the voice, and loss of voice after speaking. Parenthetically, note that should you observe this syndrome in someone (including yourself), promptly refer him to an otolaryngologist and/or a speech pathologist. The usual accompanying factors are improper breathing and incorrect adjustment of the muscles of the larynx (voice box) during speech.

Incorrect pitch of the voice is probably the most obvious voice problem we can recognize. Continuing our use of ministers for illustration, we may hear them speaking in much too high a voice, particularly while talking loudly, or in much too low a voice, in an erroneous attempt to sound more masculine and authoritative. Either habit can cause damage to the larynx. The same rehabilitation procedures as those used for loudness disorders are employed.

Quality disorders of voice include strained quality, breathiness, too much or too little nasality, and harshness. The pastor's role as counselor of individuals with such problems is to be able to report what he hears and sees in his counselees. He tells the speech pathologist what he has observed and, in some instances, his reactions. His role is to encourage the person's total involvement in the retraining of the voice, from professional diagnosis to discharge after therapy.

ORGANIC DISORDERS

There can also be voice disorders involving polyps on the vocal folds, webs between the vocal folds, ulcers on the folds, damage by caustic solutions, and structural damage from trauma. The most feared voice problem is cancer of the larynx.

The pastor-counselor's role changes completely when there has been cancer of the larynx or some other incident that necessitates the removal of the larynx. The surgery is called a laryngectomy, and the post-surgical patient is called a laryngectomee. The operation alters all aspects of the victim's life. The pastor is now dealing with a person who has lost both a critical body part and his lifelong manner of conversation.

To help see the import of it all, let us review what initially may seem unrelated. A man in his late forties was informed by the specialists in the clinic of a major university school of dentistry that he needed to have a tooth pulled. The man went into a type of shock. He felt faint and had to sit down. He perspired and shook. It was not the pain that he feared. It was the realization that he would no longer have all his teeth. He would no longer be an entire person—a whole man. He had been pleased that he still had *all* his teeth at that age. Finally he consented and the extraction was done. He went back to his own office still suffering from the event and the resulting "imperfection." Several months later he mentioned the occurrence to another dentist who was a personal friend. This dentist then explained that the man's reactions were very normal and typical. He explained that more people than the public could ever imagine react the same way. Many—both males and females—feel a castration experience, a sterility, at the time of tooth extractions. How much *more* terrible it is to face the near life-or-death alternative of having part of your neck removed or dying with cancer. No longer will any part of your life be exactly the same. One of the basic ingredients of life—communication—is permanently altered. When the patient comes back from surgery he no longer has his voice box. He no longer can speak as he has all his life. His change in communication changes his vocational, social, economic, and sometimes religious life styles.

Imagine, pastor, that you were deprived of your voice that has been the primary tool of your trade. The surgery has eliminated this distinctive and unique part of your identity. Even the shape and size of your neck is changed. The sense of smell is essentially gone, and the sense of taste is grossly modified. Perhaps you can even imagine what it would be like to no longer whisper or sing. The imagining you are doing is only a starting point for a close, personal communion with the post-laryngectomy person.

The laryngectomee feels alone, bitter, resentful, fearful, angry, frustrated, and even rejected. But the extent and intensity of these and a myriad of other feelings are limited by the counseling he receives from the medical and rehabilitation teams, his spouse and family, and you, the pastor. Be aware that you are partially responsible for the type of support (or lack of it) that he gets from the family.

Your counseling depends on your knowledge of the causes of his problem, what specifically was removed surgically, what each member of the team is doing, and *what the alternatives are* which lie ahead. Possibly one of the worst mistakes a pastor-counselor can make is proceeding with counsel without adequate knowledge, particularly when the person has lost his ability to question, debate, challenge, or even fight back verbally when he hears something he knows is wrong or hears something he needs clarified.

Now let us look at some specific areas. If the patient has been in a public contact profession, the chances are that he will have to either modify his current profession or change to a completely new one. If he has been a courtroom lawyer he can shift to a different field of law. If he has been a salesman he can change to an area in sales that demands less use of the voice. A minister could do more individual, personal work and leave the pulpit to another. In rare cases during the counseling the pastor will find that the counselee has had a real interest in a second field and the pastor can point out that this is a good time to try it out.

As in all pastor-client relationships, *let the person express his concerns.* Let him know that the concerns are legitimate, normal, and accepted as such. A wage earner has a tremendous burden suddenly laid on his shoulders. Your duty is to help him to learn how to bear it without it crushing him.

With the change of employment there is an accompanying change in income. The family usually has to adjust to a lower economic level. The degree of trauma that accompanies this is determined by the family's attitude toward the economic level to which they have been accustomed. Some families let their entire lives revolve around the display of their temporal worth. Such families become miserable comforters of the laryngectomee. On the other end of the spectrum, those already at the lower economic levels are minimally affected. Regarding the financial "new life," the pastor is to ask, "What are the available alternatives?" Do not consider alternatives that are out of reach. "What must each member of the family do to lessen the shock of the change?" "What reserves are there that will help bridge the trying times?" "What are the external sources that can be tapped?" Ask these questions and let the patient and his associates come up with the best answers. This is *not* the time to bring up tithe, church building funds, offerings, or bequests to the church. If the patient mentions them out of a deep concern, the pastor should let him express his thoughts and then state that perhaps there is a better time to discuss these things in depth.

The laryngectomee has two alternatives for future speech. The one is the use of an artificial larynx—a vibrator held against the neck; the other is esophageal speech that is done by controlled burping of air trapped in the top of the esophagus.

As we move now to the laryngectomee's social changes, the minister will observe that the patient and the spouse have their socializing cut dramatically. More often than not the old acquaintances do not wish to strain to understand the new speech. It is an effort for the new laryngectomee to use his new alternate means of speech sound production, particularly with any background noise. It is a weeding-out period. Only the true friends will stay by and walk through this dark valley with the afflicted person.

Socialization includes church attendance. It becomes too much of a chore for the laryngectomee to try to visit with others of the congregation. It is too much of a trial to be heard, to be accepted as still being a whole person, to be understood from many angles. Even pastors do not try as they should.

Laryngectomees have confrontations similar to the following: One of the writer's patients had received a head injury in an automobile accident which resulted in brain damage with symptoms like those of cerebral palsy. The patient's pastor came to visit him and, after hastily saying several things to the man, who could not respond instantly, cupped his hands to the patient's ear and shouted, "Can you hear me in there?" Such ignorance is inexcusable. Many laryngectomees tell of other people who stop talking to them and start writing, apparently feeling that if you lose your voice you must also lose your hearing.

Lastly we come to the religious life of laryngectomy patients. One of the fascinating differences about the laryngectomee is the lesser probability that he will go through a prolonged period of asking, "Why did God let this happen to me?" Hospital statistics overwhelmingly show that people who have been tobacco smokers are the majority of laryngectomees, and there is no way of blaming God for one's habit of smoking. Laryngectomees' guilt experiences are different from others in that they *know* the problem is largely their own fault. Facing God with their condition is, therefore, also different. The pastor's role is to help the client face the facts squarely, confess his sins to God in a simple, honest way, and then move on. Moralizing does not do anyone any good except as some pastors feel they have done their ministerial duty.

STUTTERING

Let us now turn our attention to stuttering. Authorities on stuttering agree that there is no one cause of stuttering, nor is there one therapy. Basically, however, they agree there are groups of theories about causes. One group maintains that stuttering is a learned behavior and another maintains that it has a neurological basis.

The three primary types of stuttering are: (1) repetitions, in which the person says the same sounds several times before being able to proceed; (2) prolongations of the initial sound which is sustained for an inordinate period of time before proceeding to the next sound; (3) blockings, in which the person is unable to initiate phonation. When these manifestations appear by themselves, they are called primary stuttering. When they are accompanied by eye blinks, facial grimaces, ticks, shrugging of shoulders, tapping of fingers, or other activities, they are called secondary stuttering. This is considered a much more severe problem. The person has to use these devices as a means of triggering the onset of speech. The most dramatic example the writer knows is a man who had to go through fourteen of these devices in a specific sequence before he could speak.

Stuttering usually begins during early childhood and in some instances can be traced to problems associated with toilet training, feeding training, discipline, conflicts in the home, a series of traumatic events, or a variety of interpersonal relationships. Numerous approach-avoidance situations can contribute to the development of stuttering. The phenomenon rarely begins at a particular moment. Rather, it develops over a period of time before being identified. According to some theories, contributing factors are penalty or punishment, fear or frustration, anger or aggression, guilt, and hostility. Another theory is known as "diagnosogenic" in which the parents and/or other persons observe normal dysfluencies that are common in all of us, interpret them as stuttering, and repeatedly inform the child, "You are stuttering," until the child lives up to it. Still another theory is that there is a hereditary or neurological predisposition to stuttering. Recently the writer has been pursuing the study of stuttering as a language-processing disorder. There seems to be evidence that the language processing when a person is acting or singing is different from the processing of volitional speech. And there is evidence that the processing for role playing is different again. Therefore, the hypothesis is that the language of a person as he stutters is processed in a different way than normal and the stuttering is the result.

Now for the pastor's responsibilities. First, T.O.T.P.—Take Off The Pressure. Allow the stuttering person to know *he is accepted* and that you will wait for him to say what he has to say and do it his way. Do not prompt him or interrupt him. Do not tell him to slow down or to think before he speaks. Maintain eye contact and listen to his message rather than to the speech disorder. Realize that he may have fears over certain sounds, words, phrases, topics, or fears of people and/or situations. He may fear either friends or strangers. A telephone frightens many people who stutter. Beyond this, the person may even fear the fear. Basically, there is a self-perpetuating factor in stuttering.

The pastor has to be the personification of compassion and is to extend it to these persons. He must work with the speech pathologist in assuring the stutterer there is neither need nor room for guilt, nor is there any reason to equate his problem with sin.

Perhaps the best closing comment on this section is to note that the stuttering person lives with assorted torments from within and an indescribable assortment of reactions from everyone else. He needs your acceptance and the assurance that God accepts him and his halting prayers, too.

ARTICULATION DISORDERS

Nearly everyone has heard a child lisp (substitute "th" for "s") in such words as "buth" for "bus" or "thun" for "sun." At first many people feel this is cute baby talk, but they soon realize it is not so cute when it is done by an older child or an adult. It can also interfere with the understanding of speech and lead to many complications in interpersonal relations.

There are four classifications of articulation disorders. The first, *substitution*, has just been illustrated. It is the use of one standard sound for another. Examples of other common substitutions are "w" for "l" as in "wake" for "lake" or "wamp" for "lamp," and "w" for "r" as in "wabbit" for "rabbit" or "wed" for "red." It is to be noted that although the pronunciation may be acoustically the same, the use of some sounds instead of others by persons coming from foreign tongues is not considered the classical substitution disorder. For example, the Japanese have no "l" sound in their native tongue. They are therefore not accustomed to using it and say "rots of ruck" for "lots of luck."

The next type of articulation disorder is the *insertion*, as is used by the person who says "helmp" instead of "help" or "potatal" for "potato." Third is the *omission* as in "pay" for "play" or "tocking" for "stocking." The fourth is *distortion*, in which the sound is not exactly what it should be, yet is not another standard sound. An example is what is called a lateral lisp, in which the sound is emitted over the sides of the tongue rather than across the middle of the front of the tongue. Another sound frequently distorted is the "l" when the tongue is not properly positioned. The "l" sound is identified but is not pure.

Not all errors in speech indicate articulation disorders. There are some instances, such as the use of "pasgetti" for "spaghetti", that the writer feels are learned and tolerated and should not be considered articulation disorders in the usual manner.

Fortunately, articulation errors are quite easily corrected with proper therapy by a speech-language pathologist. Consideration must be given, however, to the person's age, sex, and hearing acuity. We cannot easily produce speech sound that we cannot hear.

ASSORTED DISORDERS

Next we will discuss the causes of articulation disorders. In the first part of this chapter it was noted that there are organic disorders and functional disorders. The most common reasons for functional articulation disorders are unmonitored and unguided speech during the formative years along with poor speech models.

Most of the rest of the articulation disorders are due to organic problems. One of the more common is cleft palate. The person has an extra hole in the roof of his mouth that has probably been attended to by surgical and/or prosthetic approaches. Without these corrective procedures, he is unable to close off the oral cavity for the production of what are called "stop-plosives" (B, D, G, K, P, and T). For these sounds the air stream has to be completely arrested and then exploded.

When the air stream is not stopped but is rerouted through the nasal cavity, there are two kinds of articulation disorders: alternate sounds result, and the nasalizing of all sounds occurs. Usually when one of these is resolved, the other one is also.

Another cause of speech problems is cerebral palsy. There are four main types of this, but dozens of identifiable variants. Although there are some quite unique speech production problems with each type, underlying them all is a problem of voluntary movement of the speech mechanism to move into and through each sound in a smooth and easy manner to produce the desired speech. The speech can be slow, slurred, jerky, loud, soft, or inconsistent, and/or may have unusual vocal quality that adds to the difficulty of understanding it.

As the pastor works with these people he is to observe the speech as part of the entire syndrome. He should know that poor speech does not indicate mental deficit. As he does with stutterers, he needs to wait out what the person has to say.

Perhaps as much as any profession or group of people, pastors realize the overriding importance of speech, and hopefully with the reading of this chapter has come some grasp of the devastation that can come with a speech disorder. Speech is our primary means of communication, but it encompasses more than speaking and hearing.

Pastors working with speech disorders make their most significant contributions to the lives of these persons when they understand the speech problems, their causes, and their effects. The key word is always: Accept. Do not judge and do not allow others to judge or ridicule. Capitalize on the speech that can be produced.

BIBLIOGRAPHY

Barsch, R. *Counseling with Parents of Emotionally Disturbed Children.* Springfield, Ill.: Charles C. Thomas, 1970.

Berne, Eric. *Games People Play.* New York: Grove Press, 1964.

Bird, Brian. *Talking with Patients.* Philadelphia: Lippincott Co., 1973.

Bissell, N. "Communicating with Parents of Exceptional Children." In *Professional Approaches with Parents of Handicapped Children.* Edited by E. Webster. Springfield: Charles C. Thomas, 1976.

Buscaglia, L. *The Disabled and Their Parents: A Counseling Challenge.* Thorofare, N.J.: Charles B. Slack, 1975.

Cull, John G., and Hardy, Richard. *Counseling Strategies with Special Populations.* Springfield, Ill.: Charles C. Thomas, 1975.

Dawidoff, Donald J. *The Malpractice of Psychiatrists.* Springfield, Ill: Charles C. Thomas, 1973.

Falck, V. "Issues in Planning Future Programs for Parents of Handicapped Children." In *Professional Approaches with Parents of Handicapped Children.* Edited by E. Webster. Springfield, Ill.: Charles C. Thomas, 1976.

Hartbauer, R. E. *Aural Habilitation: A Total Approach.* Springfield, Ill.: Charles C. Thomas, 1978.

Hartbauer, R. E. *Counseling in Communicative Disorders.* Springfield, Ill.: Charles C. Thomas, 1978.

Iwin, R. B. *A Speech Pathologist Talks to Parents and Teachers.* Pittsburgh: Stanwix House, 1962.

King, Rella R., and Berger, Kenneth W. *Diagnostic Assessment and Counseling Techniques for Speech Pathologists and Audiologists.* Pittsburgh: Stanwix House, 1971.

Mash, E.; Handy, L.; and Hammerlynck, L. *Behavior Modification Approaches to Parenting.* New York: Brunner/Mazel, 1976.

Murphy, A. "Parent Counseling and Exceptionality: From Creative Insecurity to Increased Humanness." In *Professional Approaches with Parents of Handicapped Children.* Edited by E. Webster. Springfield, Ill.: Charles C. Thomas, 1976.

Oden, Thomas C., et al. *After Therapy What?* Springfield, Ill.: Charles C. Thomas, 1976.

Richardson, W.; Dohrenwend, B.; and Klein, D. *Interviewing: Its Forms and Functions.* New York: Basic Books, Inc., 1965.

Rogers, C. *Client-Centered Therapy.* Paper ed. Boston: Houghton-Mifflin, 1965.

Satir, Virginia. *Peoplemaking*. Palo Alto, Calif.: Science and Behavior Books, Inc., 1972.

Slovenko, Ralph. *Psychotherapy, Confidentiality and Privileged Communication*. Springfield, Ill.: Charles C. Thomas, 1966.

Sullivan, H. *The Psychiatric Interview*. New York: W. W. Norton and Co., 1954.